WORLD WILDLIFE FUND

Animal

ISBN 0-7683-2011-9

First Printing, March 1997   Second Printing, September 1997

Published by Cedco® Publishing Company, 100 Pelican Way, San Rafael, CA 94901.
For a free catalog of our entire line of books, write us at the address above
or visit our website: *http://www.cedco.com*

front cover photo: © Renee Lynn
back cover photo: © Art Wolfe
inside front cover and inside back cover photo: © Gerry Ellis Nature Photography
title page photo: © Kevin and Cat Sweeney

ABC's

A

Antelope

B

Butterfly

C

Crab

D

Dolphins

E

Elephants

F

Fox

G

Giraffes

H

Hummingbird

I

Iguana

© Cheryl A. Ertelt

J

Jaguar

K

Koala

L

Lion

M

Manatee

N

Newt

© Joe McDonald

O

Owl

© Ria Groszmann

P

Panda

Q

Quail

R

Rhinoceros

S

Seal

Toucan

U

Sea Urchin

V

ultures

© Don Getty

W

Whale

X

Ox

Y

Yak

Z

Zebra

STAR WARS
MADE EASY

WRITTEN BY CHRISTIAN BLAUVELT

CONTENTS

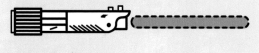

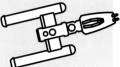

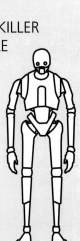

YOUR JOURNEY BEGINS HERE...

Whether you are on the dark side or the light side, these are the five steps to Star Wars knowledge...

1. YOU ARE NOT ALONE

You are not the only one who hasn't seen *Star Wars* (otherwise this guide would be pointless!)

2. START WITH THE BASICS

The Basics section gives the general lowdown on *Star Wars*. Start here, so you don't feel lost in space!

3. MOVIE BY MOVIE

Work your way through each film. We've made it easy, giving you the main plot points at a glance. You can always delve deeper once you're hooked.

4. TONGUE-TIED?

Check out the pronunciation guide and glossary at the back of the book if anything seems a little alien...

5. READY TO ROLL

You'll know your Wookiees from your wampas in no time, and be ready to dazzle friendly *Star Wars* fans with your new-found knowledge!

"Much to learn,
you still have…"

YODA

STAR WARS
THE BASICS

OK, let's start at the very beginning…

WHAT IS STAR WARS?

I know it has laser swords, a gold guy, a little green guy, and a big guy with a shiny helmet. Beyond that, you're gonna have to help me.

IS IT ABOUT SPACESHIPS?

No, it's about people. Some of them are on spaceships, but they are all caught up in a classic battle of good versus evil and trying to work out their place within it. Some turn out to be heroes, some revel in being villains, and some do both.

WHO DO I ROOT FOR?

There are brave freedom fighters in the Rebel Alliance, and noble knights called Jedi. They do battle with Sith Lords, stormtroopers, and more, but we'll get to all that. The original hero at the heart of it all is Luke Skywalker, and there are many other cool characters that follow.

Luke's journey starts on his home planet of Tatooine. Little does he know what the galaxy has in store for him…

IS IT OLD?

Well, the first movie came out in 1977 but a new trilogy of movies began in 2015 with Episode VII: *The Force Awakens*. And there are definitely more to come!

IS IT GOOD?

Yes! It's loved by millions of fans around the world for its swashbuckling style, its sense of humor, its awesome effects, and much more. If you've never seen it, treat yourself, and let us be your guide…

> **"A special effect without a story is a pretty boring thing."**
> *GEORGE LUCAS, CREATOR OF* STAR WARS

STAR WARS IS…

- A 1977 movie that spawned numerous sequels and prequels, and was later renamed *Star Wars*: Episode IV *A New Hope*.

- The big-screen saga that began in 1977, continuing through to 2017 with Episode VIII: *The Last Jedi*!

- An umbrella title for movies set in the saga universe, but based around different characters, such as those seen in *Rogue One: A Star Wars Story*.

- A multimedia phenomenon that includes two digitally animated TV series: *Star Wars: The Clone Wars* and *Star Wars Rebels*.

- Several ongoing series of best-selling books and comics telling new adventures set in the official movie universe.

- All of the above—and more!

I'm pretty sure none of this stuff is real, so...

WHO CREATED STAR WARS?

There must have been a time before Star Wars, *right? At some point in the days before Jedi and Jawas, someone had to say: "Let there be lightsabers!"*

WHO CAME UP WITH THE IDEA FOR *STAR WARS*?

In 1973, a young filmmaker named George Lucas hit the big time with *American Graffiti*, a nostalgic movie set in 1962, in his hometown of Modesto, California. The success of this film allowed Lucas to begin exploring some more unusual ideas for his next movie. He began to sketch out the basics of an outer-space adventure, which eventually became *Star Wars*.

WHERE DID GEORGE LUCAS GET HIS IDEAS?

Lucas drew inspiration from all over the place, but two big influences were the *Flash Gordon* serials of his youth and the Akira Kurosawa adventure film *The Hidden Fortress*. He was also inspired by *The Hero with a Thousand Faces* by Joseph Campbell—a book that set out to prove there was an archetypal "Hero's Journey" common to myths and legends all through history. Lucas wrote the story of Luke Skywalker's evolution from farmboy to Jedi after reading Campbell's 17-point framework.

GEORGE LUCAS

DID LUCAS WRITE AND DIRECT EVERYTHING?

He wrote and directed the first *Star Wars* movie in 1977, and wrote the stories for the next two (Episodes V and VI). Starting in 1999, Lucas also wrote and directed the entire prequel trilogy (Episodes I–III). But in 2012 he retired from blockbuster filmmaking, and Kathleen Kennedy became president of Lucasfilm, the company Lucas founded to make *Star Wars* in the 1970s. The *Star Wars* movies released since 2015 are the work of new teams building on George Lucas' legacy.

> **"I wanted to make a space fantasy."** GEORGE LUCAS

CURRENT CREATORS

KATHLEEN KENNEDY is the president of Lucasfilm and an executive producer for all 21st-century *Star Wars* movies. She also worked on all four *Indiana Jones* movies.

J.J. ABRAMS co-wrote, produced, and directed Episode VII: *The Force Awakens* and is an executive producer on Episodes VIII: *The Last Jedi* and IX.

RIAN JOHNSON wrote and directed Episode VIII: *The Last Jedi*.

COLIN TREVORROW is the co-writer and director of Episode IX.

WHO WERE LUCAS' CHOSEN FEW?

Lawrence Kasdan co-wrote screenplays for Episodes V and VI. He also co-wrote Episode VII: *The Force Awakens,* and the Han Solo stand-alone movie.

Irvin Kershner was handpicked by George Lucas to direct Episode V: *The Empire Strikes Back* in 1979. He died in 2010, aged 87.

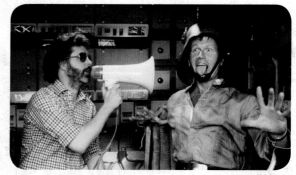

Richard Marquand was picked to direct *Return of the Jedi* after George Lucas saw his thriller *Eye of the Needle*. He died in 1987, aged 49.

There have been outer-space adventures before and since, so...

WHY IS STAR WARS SO POPULAR?

Forty years after the first film came out, people still can't get enough of Star Wars. What makes so many fans this devoted to a film series?

WHY WAS *STAR WARS* SO BIG IN THE FIRST PLACE?

When the first *Star Wars* movie came out in 1977, it tapped into a mood. After the dark days of the Vietnam War and the Watergate scandal, the against-all-odds adventures of Luke Skywalker and friends were a beacon of hope. The fact that the cast was largely unknown and the special effects were like nothing ever seen before added to a sense that this was something really new.

Star Wars was a phenomenon right from the start, with lines snaking around the block as audiences went to see it again and again!

WHY IS *STAR WARS* STILL SO BIG TODAY?

At its heart, *Star Wars* is a simple and classic tale: heroes fighting villains and learning about themselves along the way. It's a story that's been told throughout history, and will probably never get old. What makes *Star Wars* extra special is that it's set in its own enormous universe. It's a richly drawn reality where even a throwaway line can lead to new adventures—whether they take place on screen, in a spin-off novel, or in the mind of a child playing with their action figures.

Today's fans form a global community that regularly comes together for events such as *Star Wars* Celebration.

IS IT ALL ABOUT THE ACTION FIGURES?

No, but they made a big difference! Long before virtual reality and other forms of interactive entertainment, *Star Wars* was pretty much the first fictional world you could truly inhabit outside the cinema.

WHAT ABOUT THE MUSIC?

George Lucas once said sound and music count for half of any movie, and there's no doubting the impact of John Williams' timeless *Star Wars* scores. But the fact is, no single element can explain *Star Wars*' success. It's just a rare example of all the elements being carefully chosen and then coming together perfectly!

BLOCKBUSTERS

Every *Star Wars* movie is one of the highest-grossing films ever made! Here's where they stand in the all-time U.S. box office chart, with figures for Episode VIII: *The Last Jedi* still to come.

#2   Episode IV: *A New Hope*

#11 Episode VII: *The Force Awakens*

#13 Episode V: *The Empire Strikes Back*

#16 Episode VI: *Return of the Jedi*

#18 Episode I: *The Phantom Menace*

#57 *Rogue One: A Star Wars Story*

#64 Episode III: *Revenge of the Sith*

#93 Episode II: *Attack of the Clones*

Source: BoxOfficeMojo.com inflation-adjusted figures as of February 2017, with *Gone with the Wind* at #1.

Darth Vader, C-3PO, and R2-D2 set hand and footprints at the Chinese Theatre, L.A., 1977.

It's confusing—it's all futuristic, and yet it's set in the past…

WHEN AND WHERE IS STAR WARS *SET*?

The Star Wars *movies start with the words, "A long time ago in a galaxy far, far away…." but there are humans and spaceships. What's going on?*

IS *STAR WARS* SET IN THE PAST?

Yes. It takes place a long time ago, but people travel the *Star Wars* galaxy in spaceships and have all kinds of technology way more advanced than ours. Their galactic society started before our own, so they got a head start.

HOW FAR IN THE PAST IS IT SET?

Well, that's never specified with an exact date. Think of "A long time ago" as the *Star Wars* version of "Once upon a time." It's there to lend an air of poetry to the saga and clearly establish that *Star Wars* is more fantasy than science fiction.

DOES THE GALAXY HAVE A LONG HISTORY?

Oh yes. Characters talk about eras in terms like "a thousand generations," while the Galactic Republic was a planetary union that lasted for at least 1,000 years.

You've taken your first step into a larger world.

OBI-WAN KENOBI

SO WHERE IS THIS OTHER GALAXY?

It isn't set in our own Milky Way galaxy, but one that looks a lot like it. We couldn't ever reach the *Star Wars* galaxy from Earth—it's entirely fictional.

> *"Well, if there's a bright center to the universe, you're on the planet that it's farthest from."*
>
> LUKE SKYWALKER TO C-3PO, ON TATOOINE

HAS THE WHOLE GALAXY BEEN EXPLORED?

No, the Unknown Region and Wild Space are unexplored. The settled galaxy expands from the wealthy Core Worlds at its center, to the lawless Outer Rim.

The rebel fleet gathers near a protostar at the end of *The Empire Strikes Back*.

IMPORTANT PLANETS IN THE *STAR WARS* GALAXY

 TATOOINE Remote desert outpost of farmers, scoundrels, and gangsters.

 HOTH Barren ice world, good for hiding out. Watch out for Yeti-like wampas!

 BESPIN Gas giant you have to visit for the flashy, floating Cloud City.

 ENDOR Its forest moon is home to the cuddly, but feral, Ewoks.

 NABOO A picturesque planet with a network of deep-sea tunnels.

 CORUSCANT This city planet is the center of the Republic and Empire.

 JAKKU A harsh desert planet where the Empire made its last stand.

 MUSTAFAR A galactic hotspot—literally. Lava covers the entire surface.

 SCARIF This tropical paradise is the center for the Galactic Empire's top-secret research.

 GEONOSIS Arid world of rocky outcroppings and insects who are great at construction.

There are some old films, some new films, some TV stuff…

SO JUST HOW MUCH STAR WARS *IS THERE?*

I've heard people say there's no such thing as "too much Star Wars," but I'd still like a rough idea of what I'm getting myself into before we go any further.

HOW MANY *STAR WARS* FILMS ARE THERE?

So far, there have been eight chapters in the main saga. *Star Wars*: Episode VIII: *The Last Jedi* is the latest, released in theaters in 2017. In 2016, there was also *Rogue One: A Star Wars Story*, which is not part of the main saga, but does take place in the official *Star Wars* universe. A second stand-alone film, about the adventures of the young Han Solo, swaggers into cinemas in 2018.

WHAT MAKES A MOVIE PART OF THE MAIN SAGA?

The very first *Star Wars* film introduced us to Luke Skywalker, and later episodes featured him or part of his family. Any movie about the Skywalkers is part of the main saga and gets the word "Episode" in its full title.

"There are so many!"

YOUNG ANAKIN SKYWALKER

ORDER OF THEATRICAL RELEASE

EPISODE IV:
A NEW HOPE
1977

EPISODE VI:
RETURN OF
THE JEDI
1983

EPISODE I:
THE PHANTOM
MENACE
1999

1970s　　　　**1980s**　　　　**1990s**

EPISODE V:
THE EMPIRE
STRIKES BACK
1980

HOW MANY *STAR WARS* TV SHOWS ARE THERE?

There are two TV series: *Star Wars: The Clone Wars*, which ran between 2008 and 2014, and *Star Wars Rebels*, which launched in 2014, and entered its fourth and final season in 2017. Both are animated series, telling longer stories than is possible in a movie. They include familiar faces from the films, as well as a cast of new characters, including those from books and comics released since the 1970s.

STAR WARS BOOKS AND COMICS, YOU SAY?

Oh yes, there are tons of them! They tell further tales about favorite characters and introduce new ones. Marvel Comics' *Darth Vader* series is a recent example of an existing character getting a bold new spin.

YOU MENTIONED NEW CHARACTERS TOO?

Characters such as Aayla Secura, Saw Gerrera, and Grand Admiral Thrawn originally came from comics and novels and have made appearances in the TV series and *Star Wars* films. Even some new worlds and weapons have made the jump from page to screen.

As well as following Darth Maul and Darth Vader, and Ahsoka Tano from *Star Wars: The Clone Wars*, *Star Wars Rebels* features fan favorite Grand Admiral Thrawn from the novels.

EPISODE III:
REVENGE OF THE SITH
2005

EPISODE VII:
THE FORCE AWAKENS
2015

EPISODE VIII: *THE LAST JEDI*
2017

2000s

2010s

EPISODE II:
ATTACK OF THE CLONES
2002

STAR WARS: THE CLONE WARS
2008

STAR WARS REBELS
2014

ROGUE ONE: A STAR WARS STORY
2016

So there's no Earth, but there are humans, and lots of aliens…

WHO LIVES IN THE GALAXY?

The humans look like us and talk like us, the aliens range from human-like beings to giant slugs, and there is a walking furball that few can understand. What's going on?

ARE THE HUMANS THERE "US"?

You mean, did they come from Earth and have our history? No, they're in a galaxy far, far away—I thought we covered this! These humans are not related to us at all, though they are anatomically identical, which probably made casting the movies a lot easier.

DO HUMANS AND ALIENS GET ALONG?

For the most part, yes. Humans are just another species, though a very prominent one and often in positions of power. They've been living alongside other species they call aliens for thousands of years.

ARE ALL SENTIENT SPECIES TREATED THE SAME?

It varies from planet to planet, but for most of galactic history, all species have been on the same footing. Humans are one of the most populous and have colonized vast swathes of the galaxy, so other species may often be seen as minorities.

WYAAAAAA!*

Translation: "Hello!"

CHEWBACCA

ARE THERE DIFFERENT LANGUAGES?

The main spoken language of the galaxy is called Basic. All humans speak Basic, but some aliens speak other languages, such as Jawaese. Certain species are physically unable to speak Basic, like Wookiees, who don't have lips to form the sounds of it!

ARE THERE ANIMALS TOO?

Yes, but for the most part they are different from the animals we know in our galaxy. There are domestic beasts such as banthas, and monsters including giant space worms.

WHAT ARE DROIDS?

Droid is the name given to robots in the *Star Wars* galaxy. There are many different types of droids and some even have emotions, but most are effectively treated as slaves. They are bought and sold, and discriminated against by many.

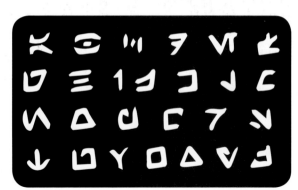

Aurebesh is the script used for the language Basic. It uses a simple 26-character alphabet.

By the time of *The Force Awakens*, the droid C-3PO is fluent in more than seven million forms of communication, and acts as an interpreter between different species.

ALIEN SPECIES TO KNOW

JAWA
Desert traders; least sinister hood-wearers in *Star Wars*

SAND PEOPLE
Masked desert warriors, a.k.a. Tusken Raiders

EWOKS
Look like teddy bears, fight like Trojans

GUNGANS
Floppy-eared warriors; targets of senseless animosity

GOOD GUYS

PADMÉ AMIDALA
Do-gooding politician,
fashion icon

BB-8
Droid co-pilot,
bundle of cuteness

C-3PO
Fussy protocol droid,
worrywart

LANDO CALRISSIAN
Scoundrel with charm
to spare

CHEWBACCA
Han Solo's best friend
and muscle

POE DAMERON
Ace pilot who buckles
and swashes

JYN ERSO
War-haunted rogue
with a rebel heart

FINN
Stormtrooper turned
"big deal" good guy

R2-D2
Robot who's man's
best friend

REY
Scavenger with a
dream… and a destiny

ANAKIN SKYWALKER
Conflicted Jedi you
don't want to cross

LUKE SKYWALKER
Farmboy, Jedi,
galactic savior

BAD GUYS

BOBA FETT
Bounty hunter with
an outsize rep

JABBA THE HUTT
Vicious, vengeful
gangster slug

DARTH MAUL
Tattooed Sith with a
double-bladed lightsaber

CAPTAIN PHASMA
Chrome-plated First
Order commander

OBI-WAN KENOBI
Jedi war hero, father
figure, bar brawler

LEIA ORGANA
Rebel leader, hair
bun aficionada

KYLO REN
First Order enforcer,
Vader wannabe

DARTH SIDIOUS
Sith Lord, Emperor,
has a bad complexion

HAN SOLO
Badass smuggler with
a heart of gold

YODA
Backward-talking
Jedi Grand Master

WILHUFF TARKIN
Snide Death Star
commander

DARTH VADER
Unstoppable force of
destruction, loves black

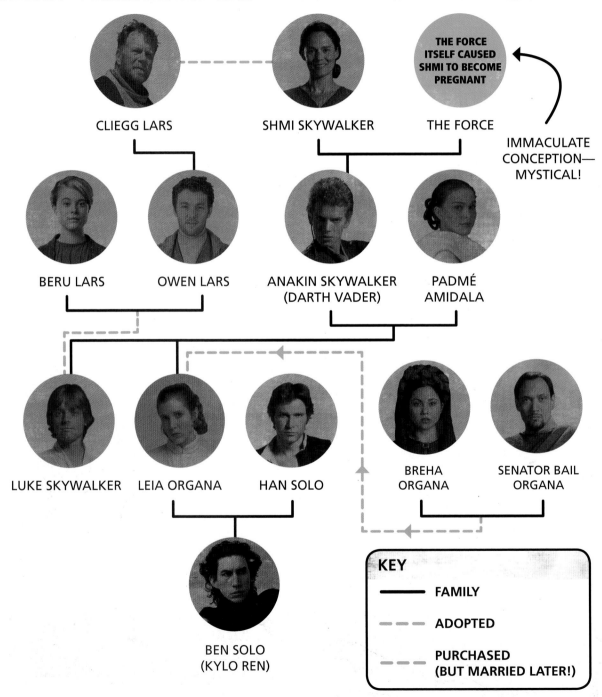

OK, *so who are all these Skywalkers...*

SKYWALKER FAMILY TREE

CLIEGG LARS

SHMI SKYWALKER

THE FORCE ITSELF CAUSED SHMI TO BECOME PREGNANT

THE FORCE

IMMACULATE CONCEPTION— MYSTICAL!

BERU LARS

OWEN LARS

ANAKIN SKYWALKER (DARTH VADER)

PADMÉ AMIDALA

LUKE SKYWALKER

LEIA ORGANA

HAN SOLO

BREHA ORGANA

SENATOR BAIL ORGANA

BEN SOLO (KYLO REN)

KEY

— FAMILY

--- ADOPTED

--- PURCHASED (BUT MARRIED LATER!)

"Looks like I'm going nowhere."
LUKE SKYWALKER

If the galaxy is so huge…

HOW DOES EVERYONE GET AROUND?

It's supposed to take at least six months to get from Earth to Mars, but in Star Wars they hop worlds like stepping stones!

HOW CAN THE SHIPS GO SO FAST?

A starship with a hyperdrive can jump from one point in space to another via a dimension called hyperspace. The difference between normal space and hyperspace is similar to the difference between a winding road and a straight one. A hyperdrive ship can reach its destination faster than the speed of light by skipping the bends of normal space.

Hold for jump to lightspeed on my go!

HOW COME THEY DON'T CRASH INTO STUFF?

Helpfully, hyperspace is pretty empty, but pilots still have to make precise calculations before a jump to lightspeed. Not only do normal space objects such as stars cast hazardous "mass shadows" in hyperspace, but also coming out of hyperspace in the wrong place could land you smack straight into a planet! Luckily, most pilots can rely on astromech droids (robots such as R2-D2) to help them navigate any obstacles.

POE DAMERON

ARE SOME SHIPS FASTER THAN OTHERS?

Definitely. Han Solo's modified freighter, the *Millennium Falcon*, is one of the fastest—partly because of its sophisticated navigation computer, but also because of its highly skilled pilots. Han boasted that he made the Kessel Run in less than 12 parsecs.

When a starship jumps to hyperspace, the stars streak into lines for one far-out lightshow.

WAIT A PARSEC...
A parsec is a real-world unit of astronomical distance equivalent to about 19 trillion miles*. So Han's boast is about his ship's ability to withstand shorter, more dangerous routes through hyperspace, rather than its speed.

*That's about
19,000,000,000,000 *miles!*

"Traveling through hyperspace ain't like dusting crops, boy!"

HAN SOLO

SOME VESSELS TO KNOW

REY'S SPEEDER
Old but sturdy and perfect for zipping around incognito.

TANTIVE IV
Princess Leia's blockade runner can take a beating.

SLAVE I
Boba Fett's ship might look like a snail in a shell, but it is considerably faster.

NABOO ROYAL STARSHIP
This glistening, mirror-surfaced ship is fit for a queen.

GEONOSIAN SOLAR SAILER
This ship uses a sail to enter hyperspace.

DEATH STAR
Even this moon-sized station has its own hyperdrive.

VEHICLES OF THE GALAXY

There's a Star Wars *vehicle* for every occasion. Whether you need to stomp over snow-covered wastes or blast away at your enemies in deep space, you'll be sure to travel in style in these magnificent machines!

MILLENNIUM FALCON
It's referred to as "a piece of junk," but Han's famous freighter is too fast for any Imperial blockade.

AT-AT
The All Terrain Armored Transport plods like a scary metal dinosaur—with laser cannons for teeth.

SNOWSPEEDER
Atmospheric fighter with tow cable perfect for tripping up AT-ATs.

TIE FIGHTER
The Empire's "twin-ion engine"—get it, TIE?—craft is speedy, but often becomes cannon fodder.

STAR DESTROYER
The odds of surviving an attack on one of these mile-long ships is very low—just ask C-3PO for the statistics!

DARTH VADER'S TIE ADVANCED X1
Vader's got style: check out those tapered wings! Plus, this craft has a hyperdrive, and a shield.

X-WING STARFIGHTER
Think *Top Gun* in space. Two Death Stars and a Starkiller Base went kablooey thanks to this workhorse.

SPEEDER BIKE
Please wear a helmet when driving these hover-cycles, especially if Ewoks are near.

The Republic, the Empire, the First Order…

WHO RULES THE GALAXY?

I thought there were two sides in Star Wars: goodies and baddies. But I get that the galaxy is a big place, so maybe it's a bit more complicated than that…

WHO IS IN CHARGE TO BEGIN WITH?

At the start of the saga, in Episode I: *The Phantom Menace*, the Galactic Republic holds sway. It's a democratic alliance of worlds, led by an elected chancellor, and protected by a noble order of knights called the Jedi. As the film begins, this era of peace has lasted 1,000 years!

BUT IT DOESN'T LAST MUCH LONGER?

How did you guess? Several planets struck out from the Republic to form their own Separatist Alliance. These Separatists were unwittingly being manipulated by the evil Sith to undermine the Republic, allowing a Sith Lord to seize control of its Senate and turn it into his own personal Empire.

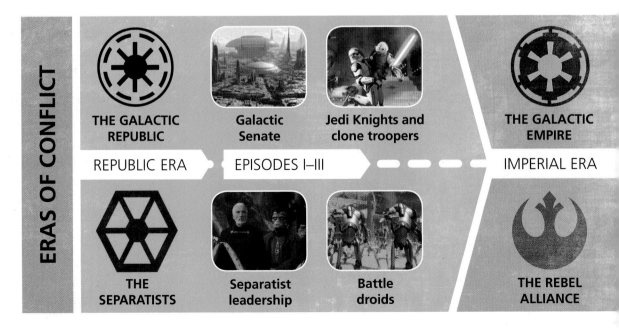

ERAS OF CONFLICT

THE GALACTIC REPUBLIC

Galactic Senate

Jedi Knights and clone troopers

THE GALACTIC EMPIRE

REPUBLIC ERA — EPISODES I–III — IMPERIAL ERA

THE SEPARATISTS

Separatist leadership

Battle droids

THE REBEL ALLIANCE

SO THE REPUBLIC IS ALSO THE EMPIRE?

Kind of… the Empire is a repurposing of the Republic by the Sith. It is made up of the same planets, but none of the same ideals. Dictatorship slowly takes the place of democracy, and by Episode IV: *A New Hope*, the last remnants of the Republic—including the Jedi—have been swept away.

WHICH IS WHERE THE REBELS COME IN?

You got it. The rebels are an alliance formed not only to bring down the Empire but also to restore the Republic. They are not out to "rule the galaxy," but when the Empire is defeated, they play a big part in the new galactic order that follows.

> ## "The Republic will be reorganized into the First Galactic Empire!"
> EMPEROR PALPATINE

WHICH IS WHAT?

The New Republic, of course! Smaller than the Empire and the old Republic that came before it, this new alliance exists peacefully alongside non-member worlds as a beacon of democracy.

SO THAT'S THE END OF THE STORY?

Nope! Thirty years after the Empire's fall, the First Order rose in opposition to the New Republic, determined to subjugate the galaxy all over again. It went to war with the New Republic—which lead to a new, rebel-style Resistance!

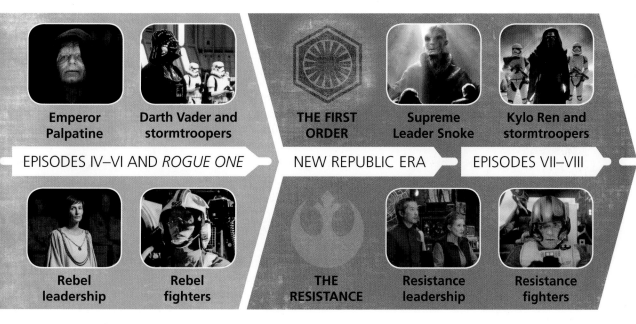

Emperor Palpatine	**Darth Vader and stormtroopers**	**THE FIRST ORDER**	**Supreme Leader Snoke**	**Kylo Ren and stormtroopers**

EPISODES IV–VI AND *ROGUE ONE*   NEW REPUBLIC ERA   EPISODES VII–VIII

Rebel leadership	**Rebel fighters**	**THE RESISTANCE**	**Resistance leadership**	**Resistance fighters**

Everyone talks about it like it's a really big deal, but...

WHAT IS THE FORCE?

Someone said I could bluff my way through a Star Wars conversation by saying, "May the Force be with you," but what does that even mean?

Force guru

SO WHAT IS IT?

The Force is a mystical energy field generated by all life forms. Some beings in the *Star Wars* universe dedicate their lives to it, but others don't even believe in it.

WHAT CAN THE FORCE DO?

With the Force, you can sense danger, levitate, and move objects with your mind, among other things. When some Force users die, they are able to return as Force ghosts. Bad guys like to use the Force to summon Force lightning, choke people from afar, and read minds.

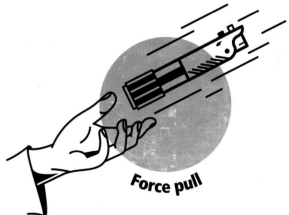

Force pull

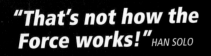

"That's not how the Force works!" HAN SOLO

IS THE FORCE USED FOR GOOD OR EVIL?

Both. The Force has a light side and a dark side. The two sides of the Force should balance each other out; the light side is used for good and the dark side for evil. Woah, this is getting deep…

Bad force

CAN ANYBODY USE THE FORCE?

No, even though all life forms generate the Force, very few beings can actually wield it. A blood test can determine your strength in using the Force. Probably best not to ask your doctor for one, though.

SO YOU'RE BORN WITH IT?

Yes, and it can run in families. If you're sensitive to the Force but haven't been trained, you can still access its power, perhaps as heightened reflexes. But you need training to be able to use it properly.

AND WHAT ABOUT THAT SAYING?

"May the Force be with you" is *Star Wars* speak for "goodbye and good luck." Next time you hear it being said, try to look sage and say, "And with you." That'll fool 'em.

MAY THE FOURTH BE WITH YOU...

The similar sound of "May the Fourth be with you" has turned May 4 every year into a semi-official "Star Wars Day," when fans around the world show their love for the franchise!

Be thankful your boss can't choke you with the Force to keep you in line.

WHO'S GOT THE FORCE?

REY—Resists mind-reading and uses telekinesis without training.

OBI-WAN KENOBI—Lightsaber-dueling is sharp, wits are even sharper.

LUKE SKYWALKER—Became an ace pilot even before training.

KYLO REN—Filled with both dark side power and doubt.

YODA—Values the Force's wisdom he does—even above warrior ways!

DARTH VADER—Possesses very strong Force abilities.

THE LIGHT SIDE

The Force flows through every living thing. If you want to live a cool, calm life, you should channel the light side of the Force in you. Don't try to impose your will on the Force—just go with the flow!

"A Jedi uses the Force for knowledge and defense, never for attack." YODA

- **WISDOM**
- **COMPASSION**
- **INNER STRENGTH**
- **LOYALTY**

POWER AND RESPONSIBILITY

The Jedi are masters of the light side of the Force. By living a strict monastic life, free from desire, they are able to wield the Force without the negative feelings that can corrupt a Force user. That means they can perform incredible feats such as telekinesis and mind tricks, but they don't have much of a laugh while they're doing it.

THE DARK SIDE

What's the point of the Force if you don't use it to have a little fun? Join the dark side if you'd rather make mischief than sit and meditate. Fuel the Force with all your rage and see what it can really do!

> *"The ability to destroy a planet is insignificant next to the power of the Force."* DARTH VADER

FORBIDDEN KNOWLEDGE

PASSION

POWER

TYRANNY

FEAR AND LOATHING

Dark side Force users choose to tap into even more destructive powers than the Jedi, but at greater cost. The Sith are the embodiment of the dark side, driven by deep emotions such as anger and fear to pursue selfish ends. As a result, every Sith is deeply twisted, and severely lacking in friends.

The Jedi are definitely the good guys, but…

WHAT IS A JEDI?

Everyone knows that they're the guys dressed in robes who carry laser swords, and everybody thinks they're the coolest. But what do they do?

> **"The Jedi Knights were the guardians of peace and justice."**
> OBI-WAN KENOBI

WHO ARE THE JEDI?

The Jedi Order is a powerful group of Force users drawn from all over the galaxy who have pledged themselves to the pursuit of peace, knowledge, and harmony with other beings. They served as the Republic's protectors and peacekeepers for thousands of years. Think of medieval knights, samurai, or the good guy Western gunslinger.

GRAMMAR NERD ALERT
The plural of Jedi is Jedi. Never "Jedis." Just like the company that makes Star Wars is Lucasfilm, not "Lucasfilms."

AND THEY HAVE LASER SWORDS?

Yes, but they're really called lightsabers. Most Jedi skills derive from the Force, including their lightsaber prowess. Other abilities include the Jedi Mind Trick, which enables a Jedi to influence the behavior of weaker-minded individuals (i.e. most people). It's sort of like hypnotism.

DO THEY HAVE A LEADER?

Yes, the Jedi Order had a Grand Master, which was Yoda, and he held that title for centuries. Yoda was the oldest and wisest of the Jedi, and he led a 12-member High Council of Jedi Masters which oversaw the Order.

YODA

WHERE ARE THEY BASED?

The main Jedi Temple is based on the Republic's city-covered capital planet, Coruscant, but they have other temples all over the galaxy.

ARE THERE LOTS OF JEDI?

Not now. The Jedi Order numbered around 10,000 Knights and Masters at the start of the Clone Wars, but the Empire and Darth Vader hunted the Jedi down, killing practically all of them.

ARE THEY MAKING A COMEBACK?

Well, sort of. Yoda trains Luke Skywalker to be a Jedi with the hope that he can recruit and develop a new generation of Jedi himself. But one of Luke's apprentices, Kylo Ren, turns against him and kills his fellow Jedi trainees (sound familiar?). So it looks like it's back to square one for the Jedi—for now…

Parents of Force-sensitive children hand them over to be trained by the Jedi.

Luke Skywalker trains young Jedi until his apprentice, Kylo Ren, turns against him.

A SELECTION OF FORCE ABILITIES

JEDI MIND TRICK—The ability to manipulate the weak-minded using the power of suggestion.

HEIGHTENED REFLEXES—Sharp reactions that aid the ability to deflect attacks with a lightsaber.

FORCE JUMP—A single massive bound that lets you scale tall barriers or deep chasms in a single bound.

FORCE PUSH—The ability to push people or objects with your mind alone.

FORCE PULL—The ability to summon objects into your hand with your mind alone.

WALK THE JEDI PATH

If you want to be a Jedi, you have to train, and train hard. It's a way of life and you have to be fully committed to the cause.

START HERE

YOUNGLING

Master Yoda himself trains the young Jedi—who are all children identified as Force-sensitive shortly after birth. They give up normal life with their parents and must sever all emotional attachments.

GRAND MASTER

The leader of the Jedi High Council, the Grand Master, is the oldest and wisest of the Jedi Masters. It is a separate role from Master of the Order (i.e. the leader of all Jedi), though both roles can be held by the same individual, as was the case with Grand Master Yoda.

PADAWAN

When a youngling has completed the Initiate Trials and built a lightsaber of their own, he or she is apprenticed to an experienced Jedi as a Padawan. They may travel—and fight—as Padawan and Master for many years.

JEDI MASTER

Promotion to the rank of Jedi Master is granted by the Jedi High Council, a body of 12 such Masters. Many choose to train a Padawan.

JEDI KNIGHT

A full-fledged Jedi is known as a Knight. To achieve this rank, a Padawan must undergo trials of teamwork, isolation, fear, anger, betrayal, focus, instinct, forgiveness, and protection.

I don't know how it works, but I want one…

WHAT IS A LIGHTSABER?

OK, firstly, they are hardly ever called "laser swords." Secondly, these super-cool weapons are powerful and tricky to master…

WHERE DO THEY COME FROM?

Jedi build their lightsabers, so each is unique to its owner. All lightsabers contain a kyber crystal—a rare gem that has a unique connection to the Force.

HOW DO THEY WORK?

Lightsabers are made up of a hilt and a plasma blade. A power cell in the hilt heats up plasma gas and focuses energy through the kyber crystal, creating the blade.

DO YOU NEED TO HAVE THE FORCE TO USE ONE?

Not necessarily, but it helps. A non-Force user can wield one, like Finn in *The Force Awakens*, but to use a lightsaber well requires great strength and control.

"An elegant weapon for a more civilized age."
OBI-WAN KENOBI

LUKE SKYWALKER

WHAT DO THE COLORS MEAN?

Lightsaber colors are determined by the color of the kyber crystal that focuses the energy beam. The Sith and other dark side Force users have red blades because they corrupt their kyber crystals, resulting in a crimson sheen. They look pretty menacing!

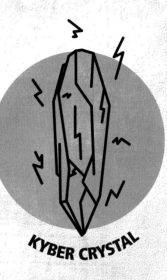

KYBER CRYSTAL

LUKE SKYWALKER

Luke builds a second lightsaber after losing his first. To hide it, he can store it inside R2-D2, who is able to shoot it out with propulsive force for Luke to catch.

DARTH VADER

This lightsaber is similar to Anakin's, but with a dark hilt and a red blade. Vader typically grips his weapon at the bottom of the hilt for powerful, slashing strokes.

DARTH MAUL

Double the blades, double the fun! This saberstaff has a hilt twice as long as usual to emit two blades—use 'em both at once or fight with one at a time.

We've talked about the good guys. What about the bad guys?

WHO ARE THE SITH?

There can be no light without the dark. And these Force users—with their all-black clothing, penchant for backstabbing, and serious rage issues—are dark.

IS A SITH AN EVIL FORCE USER?

Yes. Some Sith were initially members of the Jedi Order, and it is rumored thatthe original Sith were turncoat Jedi. To be a Sith means to reject everything the Jedi Order stands for. They pursue power instead of peace and use the dark side of the Force.

"Give yourself to the dark side." DARTH VADER

IS EMPEROR PALPATINE A SITH?

Yes. Palpatine trained exclusively under his Sith Master, Darth Plagueis, from a young age. When Palpatine became Emperor, the Sith gained total control of the galaxy.

HOW MANY SITH ARE THERE?

It is rumored that there were thousands of Sith, just like Jedi, but they constantly killed one another in their power struggles. This led to the introduction of the Rule of Two—there can only ever be two Sith at any one time: a master and an apprentice.

Kylo Ren has pledged himself to the dark side and the destruction of the Jedi, though it's unclear if he's actually a Sith.

Darth Sidious' first apprentice was Darth Maul, who he trained from childhood to be a Sith. Maul fervently follows his Master's orders.

SITH MASTERS AND APPRENTICES

DARTH PLAGUEIS
Sith Lord who
sought eternal life
and trained Sidious

DARTH SIDIOUS
a.k.a. Sheev
Palpatine, future
Emperor

3

2

1

KYLO REN
Says he's of the
Knights of Ren.
Is he a Sith?

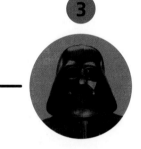

DARTH VADER
a.k.a. Anakin
Skywalker, ex-Jedi
hero of the Clone Wars

DARTH TYRANUS
a.k.a. ex-Jedi
Count Dooku, the
Separatist leader

DARTH MAUL
Sidious' first
apprentice, used
purely as a warrior

WHAT DOES "DARTH" MEAN?

Darth loosely translates to "Dark Lord," and all Sith Lords use it. They take on a new name along with "Darth." So when he turns to the dark side, Anakin Skywalker becomes Darth Vader, rather than Darth Anakin or Darth Skywalker.

SO IS THE EMPIRE JUST… THE SITH?

The Empire certainly reflects Sith teachings: it's all about accumulating power, exploiting the weak, stealing from others, and valuing war and hatred above peace. But your average stormtrooper may never even have heard of the Sith.

DO YOU KNOW

Clone troopers serve in the army of the Galactic Republic. They fight in the name of democracy, but have few individual liberties, having been bred as identical, obedient servants. Their creation paved the way for the stormtroopers.

"Your clones are very impressive. You must be very proud." *OBI-WAN KENOBI*

**PHASE I
CLONE TROOPER**
Episode II: *Attack of the Clones*

**PHASE II
CLONE TROOPER**
Episode III: *Revenge of the Sith*

**PHASE I
CLONE TROOPER**

BRED FOR WAR

For many years, the peaceful Galactic Republic needed no army and relied on the Jedi for its protection. But when the evil Sith engineered a galactic war, they also furnished the Republic with a ready-made military. Millions of genetically engineered clones served the Republic faithfully during the Clone Wars, but eventually turned on their Jedi masters.

YOUR TROOPERS?

Stormtroopers are the elite soldiers of the Galactic Empire. Clad in striking white armor, they use force and fear to impose Imperial rule and put down rebellion wherever they find it. A mighty stormtrooper army also serves the First Order.

"Stormtroopers? Here? We're in danger!" *C-3PO*

IMPERIAL STORMTROOPER
Episodes IV, V, and VI, and
Rogue One: A Star Wars Story

FIRST ORDER STORMTROOPER
Episode VII: *The Force Awakens*
and Episode VIII: *The Last Jedi*

ENLISTED IN EVIL

With limited career prospects under Imperial rule, most stormtroopers are humans who signed up willingly. Little humanity survives when they have completed their training, however, with troopers coming to think of themselves as numbers rather than names. Specialized stormtrooper units include snowtroopers, scout troopers, and death troopers.

IMPERIAL STORMTROOPER

Episode IV came out in 1977 and Episode I in 1999, so…

WHICH FILM SHOULD I WATCH FIRST?

No one can say there is a right or a wrong way to watch the Star Wars movies—each is interesting in its own right. However, the order in which you watch them can shape how you appreciate each film, and the saga as a whole.

IN-WORLD CHRONOLOGICAL

The prequels expanded the *Star Wars* galaxy and set up some of the original trilogy's most dramatic moments.

1

4

EPISODE I

RELEASE DATE

Watch the story unfold in the original order. Starting with Episode IV allows for the all-time-great twist in Episode V to have maximum impact.

1

5

EPISODE IV

OR WHY NOT TRY...

Watching Episodes IV and V first. Then watch the prequels and *Rogue One* to fill in the backstory, and finish off with Episodes VI, VII, and VIII.

PICK YOUR PATH

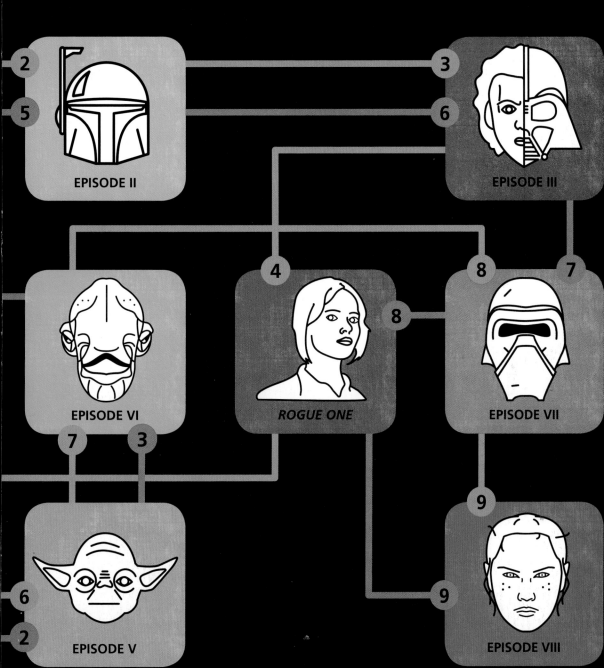

EPISODE IV:
A NEW HOPE

"Help me,
Obi-Wan Kenobi. You're
my only hope."

PRINCESS LEIA

EPISODE IV: *A NEW HOPE*
AT A GLANCE

Empire captures
Princess Leia's ship

Leia quickly hides
secret message in
R2-D2

Droids
escape in
a small
pod

R2-D2 and C-3PO

Luke's uncle
buys the
two droids

R2-D2 and C-3PO
captured by Jawas

Droids land
on Tatooine

Death Star
destroys planet
Alderaan

Luke
views the
secret
message

Obi-Wan
gives
Luke
his dad's
lightsaber

Empire
kills
Luke's
family

Luke seeks out
Obi-Wan Kenobi

Luke learns he's
the son of a Jedi

Luke, Obi-Wan,
and the droids
go to Mos
Eisley

They bargain
with Han Solo
and Chewbacca

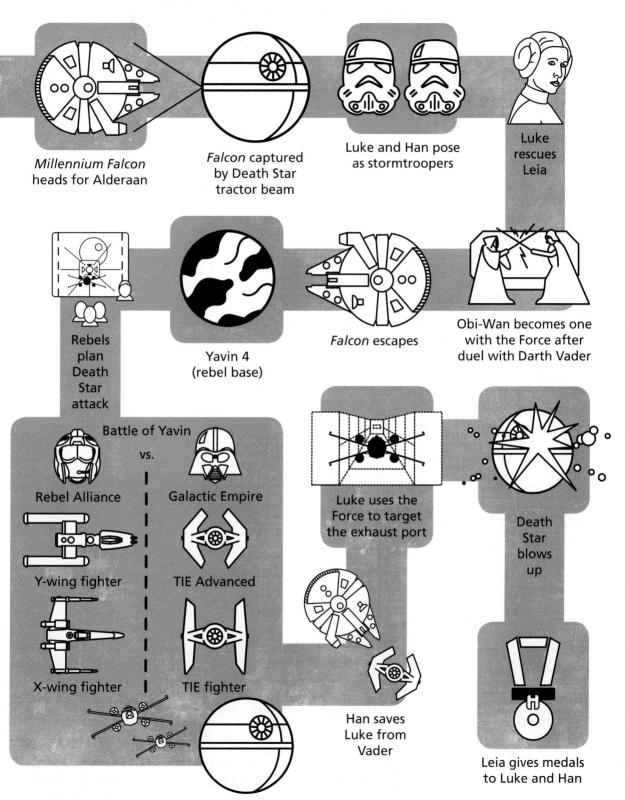

Millennium Falcon heads for Alderaan

Falcon captured by Death Star tractor beam

Luke and Han pose as stormtroopers

Luke rescues Leia

Rebels plan Death Star attack

Yavin 4 (rebel base)

Falcon escapes

Obi-Wan becomes one with the Force after duel with Darth Vader

Battle of Yavin

vs.

Rebel Alliance

Galactic Empire

Y-wing fighter

TIE Advanced

X-wing fighter

TIE fighter

Luke uses the Force to target the exhaust port

Death Star blows up

Han saves Luke from Vader

Leia gives medals to Luke and Han

49

EPISODE IV: *A NEW HOPE*
A CLOSER LOOK

Cinema in the 1970s was pretty dark, reflecting the huge social upheaval happening in America at the time. In 1977, Star Wars sliced through all the cynicism with a bright blue lightsaber, telling a swashbuckling story of good versus evil that brought back fun—and hope. On the way, it changed movies forever.

TROUBLE ON TATOOINE

An evil Empire rules the galaxy, but a band of freedom fighters seeks to bring them down. The rebel Princess Leia is captured, but not before she places a vital message and secret plans for the Death Star inside R2-D2. With fellow droid C-3PO, he sets out to deliver it to Obi-Wan Kenobi on the planet Tatooine, but circumstances lead them to a lonely farmboy named Luke Skywalker.

DESTINY CALLING

Luke sees Leia's message to Obi-Wan and seeks him out. Obi-Wan tells Luke that he is the son of a great galactic peacekeeper called a Jedi. He gives Luke his father's lightsaber, and Luke agrees to join him in helping Leia.

Luke and Obi-Wan go to Mos Eisley to find a pilot who will take them to Alderaan. There they meet Han Solo.

MEET LORD VADER

Leia is interrogated by Darth Vader, a nightmarish figure in a black mask. After she refuses to reveal the location of the secret rebel base, he has her locked up in the Empire's vast new space station, the superpowered Death Star.

OFF TO ALDERAAN

Leia's message urged Obi-Wan to go to Alderaan. But when he and Luke arrive there in Han Solo's ship, the *Millennium Falcon*, they find only the Death Star, which has totally destroyed the planet.

DRESS-UP DRAMA

Han and Luke sneak onto the Death Star disguised as stormtroopers. They rescue Princess Leia while Obi-Wan goes on his own mission to help them all escape.

Our heroes only just avoid getting crushed as garbage on the Death Star!

OBI-WAN OVER AND OUT

Giving the others time to get away, Obi-Wan faces Darth Vader in single combat. Lightsabers clash, but once Obi-Wan sees that his friends are safe, he lets himself be struck down. Luke is devastated.

A PLAN BUT NO HAN

Luke, Han, and Leia reach the rebel base on Yavin 4. The plans inside R2-D2 reveal a fatal flaw in the Death Star's design. The rebels plan to attack it, but Han opts to leave.

HOPE HAS WINGS

The rebels attack in small fighters, and Darth Vader goes after Luke in his own ship. At the last moment, Han joins the fight in the *Falcon*, saving Luke. Luke hears Obi-Wan's voice telling him to use his instincts and the Force, not his computer, to destroy the Death Star. He succeeds and brings new hope to the galaxy!

GOOD GUYS

LUKE SKYWALKER
Farmboy destined to feel the Force

HAN SOLO
Smug smuggler with a fast ship

PRINCESS LEIA
Rebel leader, hairstyle icon

OBI-WAN KENOBI
Jedi and Leia's only hope—a.k.a. Ben Kenobi

C-3PO and R2-D2
Droid pals on a mission

CHEWBACCA
Han's co-pilot and BFF—a.k.a. Chewie

BAD GUYS

DARTH VADER
The Empire's shiniest Sith Lord

GRAND MOFF TARKIN
Death Star top dog

So I know this film was released first, but…

WHY DOES STAR WARS START WITH EPISODE IV?

I sat down with my popcorn, ready to start at the beginning, and the intro said "Episode IV." Am I watching the right movie?

WHY START IN THE MIDDLE OF A STORY?

The young George Lucas was a guy with a lot of ideas! His original story for _Star Wars_ was so long, it could never fit into a single movie, so he had to pick one part to focus on.

BUT WHY EPISODE IV?

Episode IV is the start of Luke's journey—when he learns about the Jedi, the Empire, and the Rebellion. His learning curve makes a great way in for an audience, too. It also takes place after the epic Clone Wars, which would have been impossibly expensive to show in 1977.

WEREN'T PEOPLE PUT OFF BY THE TITLE?

No one in 1977 was worried that they'd missed Episodes I–III, as the Episode IV tag wasn't added until the movie was re-released in 1981. By that time, Lucas had already called its sequel Episode V: _The Empire Strikes Back_.

LUKE SKYWALKER

HOW DID GEORGE LUCAS KNOW HE'D NEED THREE PREQUEL EPISODES?

By the time he added Episode IV to the title, Lucas knew the structure of the prequel story he wanted to tell. He wasn't sure it would ever happen, though.

WHY WAIT SO LONG TO MAKE THE PREQUELS?

Mostly, George Lucas was just waiting for technology to catch up with his imagination. He founded the company Industrial Light & Magic (ILM) to make the visual effects for *Star Wars* in 1975. By the 1990s, ILM was creating digital effects for films such as *Jurassic Park*, convincing Lucas it was time to show the Galactic Republic in all its glory—city planets, clone armies, and all!

WAS *THE FORCE AWAKENS* PLANNED IN THE 1970s?

No, both Episode VII: *The Force Awakens* and Episode VIII: *The Last Jedi* are the products of brand new creative teams.

Episode IV sets up intriguing mysteries by not showing everything from the start—such as how do Obi-Wan and Vader know each other?

Episodes I–III use vast battle droid and clone trooper armies, while Episode IV only calls for stormtrooper squads.

AN INTRODUCTION TO...

THE EMPIRE—Tyrannical regime that rules the galaxy from very, very big starships.

THE REBEL ALLIANCE—Freedom-lovers who do their best to bring down the Empire.

IMPERIAL SENATE—A remnant of better times, this Senate operates under the Empire.

PRINCESS LEIA—Young Imperial Senator who secretly helps lead the Rebel Alliance.

THE DEATH STAR—Moon-sized ultimate weapon, newly completed by the Empire.

THE DEATH STAR PLANS—Stolen battle station blueprints vital to the rebel cause.

WHY IS OBI-WAN LEIA'S ONLY HOPE?

Leia sends a message to Obi-Wan Kenobi before she gets caught by the Empire. Why does she do that when she's never even met the guy?

Help me, Obi-Wan Kenobi...

WHY NOT CONTACT THE OTHER REBELS?

The Empire is hot on Leia's heels. She knows that a transmission or a small ship sent in the direction of the rebel base will be detected and will give away their hiding place. She also knows that, as the ship is right above the planet Tatooine where Obi-Wan Kenobi lives, Darth Vader may be led straight to him.

IS THAT JUST LUCK?

No. Leia was headed there to recruit Obi-Wan to the rebel cause. She sends him a message when she can't get to him in person.

WHAT DOES SHE SEND TO OBI-WAN?

Along with her message, Leia has placed the stolen plans for the Death Star in the memory of droid R2-D2. As revealed in the 2016 film, *Rogue One: A Star Wars Story*, she received those plans just moments before, at great cost to the Rebel Alliance.

LEIA ORGANA

WHY SEND R2-D2?

Leia is cornered and ingeniously makes use of what she has at hand. Also, she knows no one will suspect a droid. The escape pod R2-D2 takes to Tatooine is ignored by the Empire because their scanners do not detect any life forms on board.

WHY SEND C-3PO?

It's not entirely clear if that is part of Leia's plan, but R2-D2 insists on bringing his friend along for the escape-pod ride!

When he meets Luke, Obi-Wan acts as if he doesn't recognize the droids, despite knowing them when he was younger (as shown in Episodes I–III). It's far from the biggest secret he's hiding, though!

IS LEIA'S FAITH IN OBI-WAN JUSTIFIED?

Definitely. As soon as she asks him to go to Alderaan, he's packing his bags! He doesn't make it, because the planet is destroyed, but instead is instrumental in freeing her from the Empire, and even sacrifices his life so she can deliver the Death Star plans herself. Leia's "only hope" also brings Luke to the fight— the "new hope" of the movie's title.

JOURNEY OF THE DEATH STAR PLANS

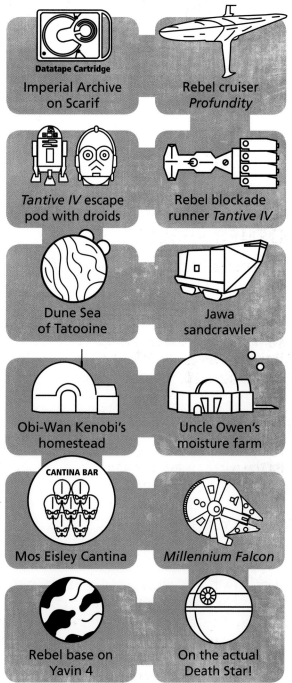

Datatape Cartridge

Imperial Archive on Scarif

Rebel cruiser *Profundity*

Tantive IV escape pod with droids

Rebel blockade runner *Tantive IV*

Dune Sea of Tatooine

Jawa sandcrawler

Obi-Wan Kenobi's homestead

Uncle Owen's moisture farm

CANTINA BAR

Mos Eisley Cantina

Millennium Falcon

Rebel base on Yavin 4

On the actual Death Star!

Everybody cares so much about its blueprints, but...

WHAT IS THE DEATH STAR?

Leia and the rebels are determined to destroy the Death Star. But what's so important about this thing?

> **"That's no moon. It's a space station."**
> *OBI-WAN KENOBI*

IS IT A PLANET?

No. The Death Star is a mobile, sphere-shaped battle station the size of a small moon.

SO WHY WAS IT BUILT?

The Death Star is the ultimate expression of the Empire's desire to dominate the galaxy and rule by fear. It has a dish that can fire a superlaser capable of destroying an entire planet. So that's why the rebels are keen to destroy it.

HOW BIG IS THE DEATH STAR?

Big! It can station about 1.5 million people: support crew and technicians, army and naval officers, starfighter pilots, and stormtroopers. Entire Imperial Star Destroyers, which are massive spaceships, are tiny in comparison.

IS THE EMPIRE BASED THERE?

Despite the number of personnel stationed on the Death Star, most of the Empire's government is based on Coruscant—the galactic capital planet.

CAN IT MOVE?

It may not look it, but it's fully mobile and can enter hyperspace just like any smaller craft. It has to be able to move around because its superlaser has a pretty limited range.

HOW POWERFUL IS THE SUPERLASER?

Well, it reduces the planet Alderaan to rubble so it's pretty powerful! The superlaser is made using kyber crystals, the same stuff that powers lightsabers, but in much greater quantities.

Death Star radius
100 miles (160 km)

PLACES DESTROYED BY THE DEATH STAR

JEDHA CITY—An arid wasteland that can't catch a break. It's stripped of its kyber crystals then blasted to dust.

IMPERIAL ARCHIVE FACILITY—The Empire destroyed it in an to attempt to keep the Death Star plans secret.

ALDERAAN—The entire planet was destroyed as a test of the superlaser at full strength.

WHO SHOT FIRST?

In a fan-favorite scene in Episode IV, Han Solo blasts a green alien named Greedo, but people swear they saw Greedo try to shoot him first. How is this even a controversy?

Greedo should have worked on his aim if he wanted to cash in on the bounty.

HAN SHOT FIRST!

Greedo's been sent to get the money Han owes to Jabba the Hutt. Han can't pay, and knows Greedo will kill him, so he has no choice but to act first in preemptive self-defense.

That, at least, was the interpretation of most *Star Wars* viewers until 1997. The scene as shot cuts to a close-up on Greedo, so it's impossible to tell if he fires at all before he meets his fate. But then came the Special Edition...

"I don't know and I don't care!"
HARRISON FORD (ACTOR PLAYING HAN SOLO)

GREEDO SHOT FIRST!

Greedo says he's come to collect Jabba's money, but that's just a ruse to put Han off his guard. At the first opportunity, Greedo tries to kill Han, misses, and is felled by Han's lightning-fast comeback.

For 1997's Special Edition re-release of Episode IV, George Lucas added extra frames to the wide shot, clearly showing Greedo firing first. For the 2004 DVD release, a futher edit made the two shots nearly simultaneous. Lucas has said it was always his intention that Greedo fires first.

"Why did you fry poor Greedo?"

JABBA THE HUTT TO HAN SOLO

ANSWER IN A NUTSHELL

It depends which version of the movie you see first! Whichever you choose to believe, the only movie version now available makes clear that Han isn't meant to be a cold-blooded killer.

He's one of the most iconic villains in movie history, but…

WHO IS DARTH VADER?

OK, Darth Vader is one of the things I definitely know about Star Wars. But then again, what does he actually do and what's with the scary mask?

HE'S PRETTY BAD, RIGHT?

Darth Vader is the ultimate embodiment of cinematic villainy. He breathes heavily through a mask, he speaks tersely, he backs up his threats, he is a master swordsman, and he chokes the life out of his subordinates on a whim. He's an icon, but perhaps not boss of the year.

DOES HE RULE THE EMPIRE?

No, Emperor Palpatine rules the Empire, but Palpatine is Darth Sidious, Lord of the Sith, and Vader is his Sith apprentice. Think of Vader as the Empire's chief enforcer—he doesn't rule, but he intimidates the galaxy into toeing the Imperial line.

SO HE ONLY ANSWERS TO PALPATINE?

Almost. Grand Moff Tarkin is the commander of the Death Star and one of the very few people in the Empire who happens to rank higher than Vader. On the Death Star, Tarkin is the ultimate authority.

DARTH VADER

WHAT'S WRONG WITH HIS BREATHING?

Vader wears a mask and suit of armor, and has his breathing mechanically regulated, because he was horribly mutilated in a lightsaber duel that took place before the events of Episode IV.

"There will be no one to stop us this time!"

DARTH VADER

WHAT DO WE KNOW ABOUT VADER'S PAST?

We know that Darth Vader was once, in fact, a Jedi and Obi-Wan Kenobi's apprentice. Obi-Wan explains that Darth Vader killed Luke's father, who was a Jedi like Obi-Wan and Vader before his fall to the dark side. This is all true… from a certain point of view. The prequels reveal the answers and tell the story of how Darth Vader fell to the dark side.

Vader lives in a castle on the planet Mustafar, as seen in *Rogue One*.

The ex-Jedi also happens to be a great starfighter pilot. It's good for a leader to be hands on!

SOME IMPORTANT IMPERIALS

TARKIN—Commander of the Death Star, pretty sure of himself.

TAGGE—Army general, Death Star skeptic, smart guy.

MOTTI—Death Star evangelist who doesn't always see eye to eye with Vader.

BAST—Officer who wanted Tarkin to evacuate the Death Star.

CASS—Guy who gives bad news to Tarkin. And there is a lot.

YULAREN—Clone Wars veteran.

Obi-Wan and Vader seem evenly matched in battle, so…

WHY DOES OBI-WAN SACRIFICE HIMSELF?

Obi-Wan seems to be winning the climactic duel with Darth Vader, even calling his opponent "only a master of evil." But then—shocker—he just gives up. Why?

DID HE JUST DISAPPEAR?

Yes, Obi-Wan's body vanishes wholesale when Vader's blade hits him. Only his Jedi robe is left. Even Vader seems shocked by that, since he stomps his foot on Obi-Wan's empty garments to see if anything is left.

UH, WHERE DID HE GO?

Oh, he was killed alright, but Obi-Wan also became "one with the Force." This means his very being merged with the Force itself. Having left this plane of existence, he still possesses his consciousness and can even talk to the living. Pretty crafty.

If you strike me down, I shall become more powerful than you can possibly imagine.

Obi-Wan's vanishing act proves the mysterious power of the Jedi, horrifying Luke and even astonishing Vader.

After Obi-Wan's death, Luke hears his voice at a critical moment, urging him to trust the Force, not his targeting computer.

SO, HE'S LIKE A GHOST?

Yup. During the Battle of Yavin Luke hears Obi-Wan's disembodied voice telling him, "Use the Force, Luke. Let go, Luke." He can still help Luke, perhaps even more effectively without his aging body.

SO HE IS MORE POWERFUL AFTER DEATH?

In a way. Now he can be anywhere and everywhere. Obi-Wan understands that it is his destiny to inspire Luke to take his place in the fight against Vader and become a symbol of Jedi peace in the face of terrible violence. You'll see how Luke adopts a similar strategy at the end of Episode VI: *Return of the Jedi*.

CAN ALL JEDI DO THIS?

Not even close. In fact, hardly any ever have. Obi-Wan's Master, Qui-Gon Jinn, was the first to manifest as a consciousness after death. He went on to train Yoda and Obi-Wan in the spooky art of non-corporeal existence.

CAN YOU BECOME ONE WITH THE DARK SIDE OF THE FORCE?

If it's possible, no one has ever managed it! Dark side Force users make the mistake of trying to preserve a physical form at all costs. They are too greedy to give up their living bodies in search of something more spiritual.

BATTLE OF YAVIN
MADE SIMPLE

INFO BOX

LOCATION—Space, just out of range of jungle moon Yavin 4

KEY BATTLE ZONE—Trench on the Death Star's surface

FORCES—Rebel Alliance and Imperial fleet

It's the ultimate David and Goliath showdown: a handful of battered rebel starfighters take on a battle station the size of a moon. But raw power alone isn't always everything.

WHO'S FIGHTING WHO?
The Rebel Alliance is taking the fight to the Empire. They have the blueprints for the Death Star, they've identified a weakness they can exploit, and this is their chance to destroy it.

REBELS

X-WINGS

MILLENNIUM FALCON

WHY ARE THEY FIGHTING?
The Death Star is zeroing in on Yavin 4 with the intent to destroy the rebel base there. The rebels must act first before it's too late.

Y-WINGS

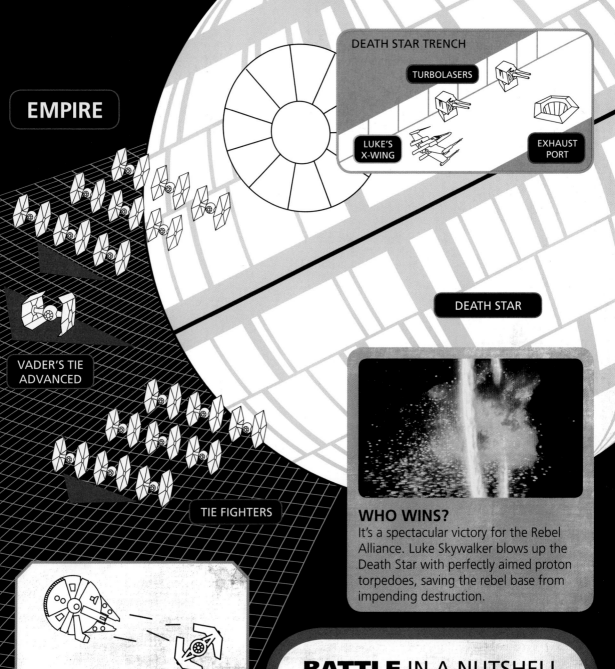

EMPIRE

DEATH STAR TRENCH

TURBOLASERS

LUKE'S X-WING

EXHAUST PORT

DEATH STAR

VADER'S TIE ADVANCED

TIE FIGHTERS

WHO WINS?

It's a spectacular victory for the Rebel Alliance. Luke Skywalker blows up the Death Star with perfectly aimed proton torpedoes, saving the rebel base from impending destruction.

KEY MOMENT

HAN SOLO ARRIVES—While Luke is flying through the Death Star's trench with Darth Vader in pursuit, Han, in the *Millennium Falcon,* returns to help Luke complete the mission.

BATTLE IN A NUTSHELL

It was the proton torpedo blast heard around the galaxy. Not only did the Death Star's destruction strike a blow to the heart of the Empire, it also inspired more worlds to join the Rebel Alliance.

EPISODE V:
THE EMPIRE STRIKES BACK

"No, I am your father."

DARTH VADER TO LUKE SKYWALKER

EPISODE V: *THE EMPIRE STRIKES BACK* AT A GLANCE

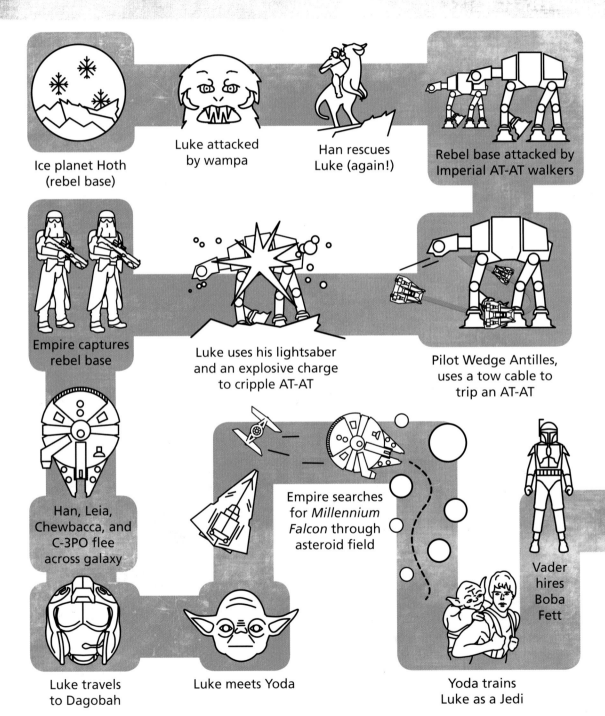

Ice planet Hoth (rebel base)

Luke attacked by wampa

Han rescues Luke (again!)

Rebel base attacked by Imperial AT-AT walkers

Empire captures rebel base

Luke uses his lightsaber and an explosive charge to cripple AT-AT

Pilot Wedge Antilles, uses a tow cable to trip an AT-AT

Han, Leia, Chewbacca, and C-3PO flee across galaxy

Empire searches for *Millennium Falcon* through asteroid field

Vader hires Boba Fett

Luke travels to Dagobah

Luke meets Yoda

Yoda trains Luke as a Jedi

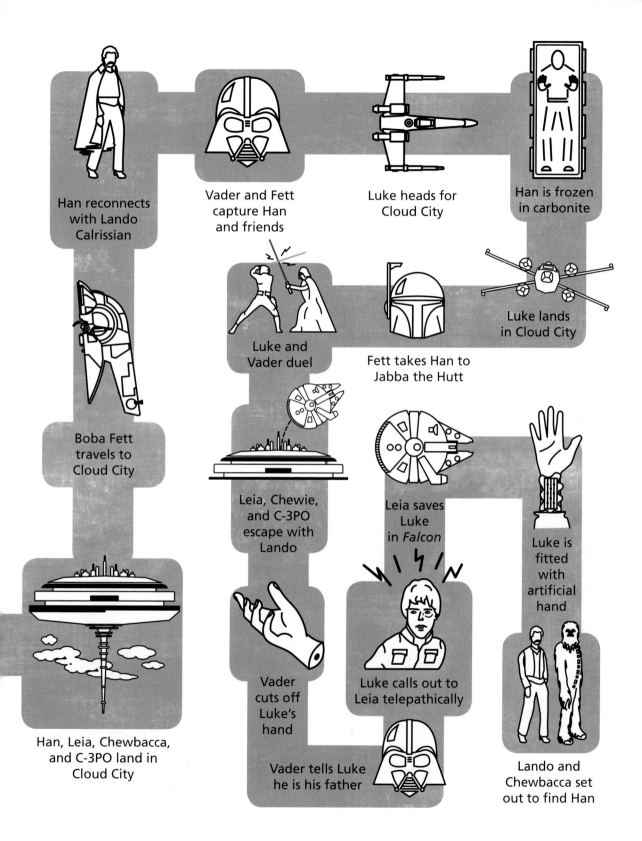

Han reconnects with Lando Calrissian

Vader and Fett capture Han and friends

Luke heads for Cloud City

Han is frozen in carbonite

Luke and Vader duel

Fett takes Han to Jabba the Hutt

Luke lands in Cloud City

Boba Fett travels to Cloud City

Leia, Chewie, and C-3PO escape with Lando

Leia saves Luke in *Falcon*

Luke is fitted with artificial hand

Vader cuts off Luke's hand

Luke calls out to Leia telepathically

Han, Leia, Chewbacca, and C-3PO land in Cloud City

Vader tells Luke he is his father

Lando and Chewbacca set out to find Han

EPISODE V: *THE EMPIRE STRIKES BACK* A CLOSER LOOK

A New Hope shattered box-office records and snagged seven Oscars. How do you top that? Not by going bigger, but by going deeper and darker. The Empire Strikes Back *introduced new characters, new worlds, and the single most famous plot twist of all time. It didn't just meet expectations, it shattered them.*

ICE COLD

The rebels have made their base on the ice planet Hoth. After a scrape with a Yeti-like wampa, Luke collapses in the frozen wastes, where Obi-Wan's Force ghost tells him to seek out a Jedi Master called Yoda.

HOTH ON THEIR HEELS

Narrowly escaping the Empire, Luke goes in search of Yoda on the planet Dagobah, while Han, Leia, and Chewie hide out in an asteroid field. Or, to be more precise, in a giant worm in an asteroid field!

THE BATTLE OF HOTH

Soon after Han rescues Luke, the Empire launches an attack on their base. The rebels battle AT-ATs—the Empire's huge, walking tanks—but are eventually forced to flee the planet.

JEDI MASTER, HE IS

On Dagobah, Luke meets a green oddball who talks backward. This is Yoda! He agrees to train Luke as a Jedi, and sends him into a cave to face the dark side. In the cave, Luke has a vision of his own face beneath Vader's mask, and realizes he must control his emotions.

Ingenious rebel pilots use tow cables to trip up AT-AT walkers on the barren surface of planet Hoth.

"How will I know the good side from the bad?" LUKE SKYWALKER

FORECAST: CLOUDY

Han, Leia, Chewie, and C-3PO make it to Cloud City, where Han hopes his old friend Lando, who runs the place, can help them. But Vader got to Lando first and forces him to trick his friend Han into a trap.

On Cloud City, Vader threatens Lando if he doesn't cooperate, and permits Boba Fett to take the captive Han to Jabba the Hutt.

"NO, *I* AM YOUR FATHER."

Vader carbon-freezes Han and gives him to bounty hunter Boba Fett. Luke senses that Leia and Han are in trouble and leaves Yoda to go rescue them, without finishing his training. He crosses sabers with Vader, loses a hand, and learns that the Dark Lord is his father. "Nooooo!"

ESCAPE ARTISTS

Vader wants Luke to join him so they can rule as father and son. But Luke doesn't want in on the family business, and throws himself into an abyss. Leia senses he is in danger, and flies to his rescue in the *Millennium Falcon*—piloted by Lando, who has come good. Later, they resolve to rescue Han.

GOOD GUYS

LUKE SKYWALKER
Jedi in training, overconfident

HAN SOLO
Lover, fighter, carbon-frozen

LEIA ORGANA
Skeptical about frenemies

LANDO CALRISSIAN
Ultimate frenemy, winning smile

YODA
Jedi Master, wisdom dispenser

OBI-WAN KENOBI
Deceased Jedi turned helpful ghost

BAD GUYS

DARTH VADER
Former Jedi, desperate father

BOBA FETT
Cool-looking bounty hunter

The movie's just started and it sure looks cold…

PLANET HOTH: REBEL BASE

Beware, all ye who want to hide out from the Empire here. Sure, a remote ice planet seems like a good place for a secret base, but Yeti-like wampa run amok and temperatures get pretty chilly to say the least. Bring a sweater!

WHY ARE THEY ON HOTH?

After the Empire discovered their base on Yavin 4 in *A New Hope*, the rebels have no choice but to move on. The seemingly uninhabitable world of Hoth provides the perfect cover for a new HQ. An asteroid field adds an extra layer of security for the rebels—it is notoriously hard to navigate.

Han uses a dead tauntaun as a sleeping bag for Luke, in a desperate attempt to keep him warm and alive.

HOW COLD IS IT?

It gets so far below freezing at night on Hoth that even the native tauntauns can die from hypothermia.

HOW DO THE REBELS GET AROUND?

Since the whole planet is covered in ice and snow, hovering snowspeeders come in handy, as do AT-AT walkers—if you have an Empire-size budget. Otherwise, a tauntaun will do.

ARE THERE ANY OTHER ANIMALS ON HOTH?

As well as tauntauns, the rebels need to look out for giant wampa. Despite their size, wampa blend into the snow with their white fur. When Luke is captured by a wampa he wakes up upside down in a cave! Using the Force, Luke manages to summon his lightsaber into his hand, cut himself free, and wound the wampa before escaping.

HOTH SURVIVAL KIT

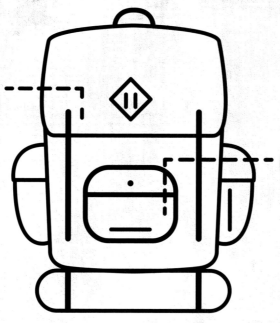

Thermal clothes
Cozy and
camouflaging

Electrobinoculars
Don't look directly
at the snow!

EXTRA EQUIPMENT

Snowspeeder
Harpoon and
tow cable included

Tauntaun
Mount and makeshift
sleeping bag

Ion cannon
Can even disable
Star Destroyers

Bacta tank
For rapid healing
after wampa attack

AVOID AT ALL COSTS

Probe droid
Watch out for these
flying spies

AT-AT
Imperial war
machines

Wampa
Vicious creatures,
will attack anything

Snow storm
You thought it couldn't
get any colder…

It all gets a little bit trippy at this point…

WHAT DOES LUKE'S VISION MEAN?

On Dagobah, Yoda takes Luke to a cave where the dark side is strong. Inside, he battles Vader—only to find his own face beneath the Dark Lord's mask! What does it all mean?

> **"The cave. Remember your failure in the cave."**
> YODA

IS DARTH VADER REALLY THERE?

No, it's just a vision. Like any hero's journey, Luke's is as much a voyage of personal discovery as it is a physical adventure. Who is he really? What is he capable of? What could he become? When Luke sees himself behind Vader's helmet, he realizes he has the potential to fall to the dark side, just like Vader.

IS THIS PART OF YODA'S TRAINING?

Yoda tests Luke by taking him to the Cave of Evil. At that point, Luke is drawn to it and makes his own decision to go inside. The Force is everywhere, and dark side energy is especially abundant in that cave, making it a pretty trippy place to visit.

WHY DOES YODA SAY LUKE FAILED?

Yoda tells Luke that all he will find in the cave is what he takes with him. That turns out to be fear and a willingness to lash out with a lightsaber. Yoda knows that Luke will need more self-control to resist the dark side. Yoda acknowledges his failure to help Luke understand what is required of a Jedi.

Luke sees himself in Vader's helmet during a Force-fueled vision on Dagobah.

IS THE VISION A CLUE TO VADER'S IDENTITY?

It works on a couple of different levels. It certainly hints at Vader being Luke's father. It also suggests that Luke should try to put himself in Vader's shoes. But mostly, it shows how Luke has the potential to fall to the dark side, too.

DOES IT OFFER A WAY TO DEFEAT VADER?

Yes, and it's not what Yoda thinks. (Even Yoda can be wrong!) The vision suggests that, on some level, Luke sees himself in Vader. Yes, Luke could fall to the dark side, but perhaps Vader could also be brought back into the light.

BEST MYSTERIOUS VISIONS

Episode V: *The Empire Strikes Back*
Luke's vision is key to the saga's message that violence is ultimately self-destructive.

Episode V: *The Empire Strikes Back*
Leia has a vision of Luke's plight when he is in danger on Cloud City.

Episode III: *Revenge of the Sith*
Anakin has a premonition that his wife, Padmé, will die.

Episode VII: *The Force Awakens*
Rey has a vision of the past when she touches Luke's lightsaber on Takodana.

I don't know if I'm supposed to love him or hate him…

WHO IS LANDO CALRISSIAN?

He's supposed to be Han's friend but he betrays the rebels, hands them over to Vader, and lets Han get frozen in carbonite. Some friend!

HOW DID LANDO GET TO RUN A WHOLE CITY?

When we meet Lando he is the Baron Administrator of Cloud City, a sprawling gas-mining facility floating above the gas giant planet, Bespin. Lando won control of the city in a card game called sabacc.

SO IS HE A SMUGGLER?

Smuggling would require getting his hands a little too dirty. Lando's more of a con man, a gambler, and even a gentleman thief. He's a former owner of the *Millennium Falcon*—he lost the ship in a card game to Han.

WHY DOES LANDO CARBON-FREEZE PEOPLE?

Lando doesn't make a habit of freezing people in carbonite. The whole facility exists to preserve the valuable gas harvested from Bespin and processed on Cloud City. Vader just happened to get a little bit creative with the technology.

You truly belong with us here in the clouds.

LANDO CALRISSIAN

Lando is slick while Han is rough around the edges. The former owner of the *Millennium Falcon* is one smooth talker.

Lando doesn't like being used by the Empire and betraying his friends. After Han is frozen, he checks to see if his poor pal survived the process.

Lando can be loyal to his friends, like the way he's stuck by old pal Lobot—except when he leaves him behind on Cloud City!

It does seem pretty strange that Lando has to wear Han's clothes after he's fled Cloud City, but he did leave in a hurry.

WAS HIS BETRAYAL OF HAN JUSTIFIED?

Well, kind of. See it from Lando's point of view: he's responsible for the lives of the thousands of people on Cloud City. Then Vader and the Empire show up and threaten everyone, unless Lando hands over his friends. He betrays Han for the greater good of the people on Cloud City.

WHY IS HE WEARING HAN'S OUTFIT AT THE END?

It's been suggested that the outfit is the remnant of a flight uniform, and so a natural choice for any pilot. But really, what better way for the filmmakers to suggest that Han is really gone than to set Lando up as his replacement, complete with his ship and fashion sense?

BATTLE OF HOTH
MADE SIMPLE

Did you really think the Empire was going to let the Death Star's destruction go unavenged? And they know revenge is best served cold.

WHO'S FIGHTING WHO?
The Empire tracks down the rebels at their new base on Hoth. The rebels evacuated their Yavin 4 base following the Death Star's destruction.

WHY ARE THEY FIGHTING?
The Empire wants to crush the Rebellion once and for all, capture its leaders, and attempt to lure Luke Skywalker to the dark side.

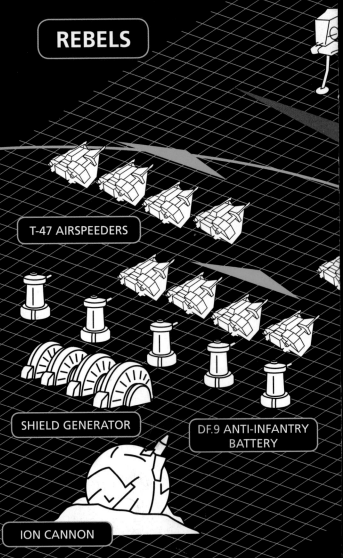

REBELS

T-47 AIRSPEEDERS

SHIELD GENERATOR

DF.9 ANTI-INFANTRY BATTERY

ION CANNON

EMPIRE

AT-AT WALKERS

AT-ST WALKERS

SNOWTROOPERS

REBEL TROOPERS

SHIELD ZONE

KEY MOMENT

JUST TRIPPIN'—Luke realizes they can take down AT-ATs by firing a harpoon attached to a tow cable and wrapping the cable around the walker's legs so it trips and falls. Wedge Antilles executes Luke's idea to eliminate the first AT-AT.

WHO WINS?
On paper, the Empire—no doubt about it. They force the rebels to abandon their base and scatter across the galaxy, leaving them more vulnerable than ever. On the other hand, a fair amount of the rebels do get away…

BATTLE IN A NUTSHELL
The Empire scored a massive psychological victory in destroying the rebels' new base. But it didn't end the Galactic Civil War—it just set up another showdown, since Luke, Leia, Han, and most of the rebels evacuated safely.

79

DARTH VADER'S BIG REVEAL

It's now famous as one of the biggest twists in movie history. But when audiences flocked to The Empire Strikes Back in 1980, they had no idea of the surprise that lay in store: Darth Vader (wait for it) is Luke Skywalker's father! No, really!

GIVE ME YOUR HAND

Luke and Vader waste no time before clashing in lightsaber combat. The Dark Lord finds his opponent "most impressive" but quickly bests the not-quite-Jedi, cutting his dueling hand clean off!

When Luke loses his hand, he also loses his father's lightsaber, given to him by Obi-Wan Kenobi.

IN THE CLOUDS

When Luke senses that Han and Leia are in danger on Cloud City, he goes there to face Darth Vader. Having skipped out of his Jedi training, he arrives under-prepared and overconfident.

WHY IT MATTERS

Misquoted or not, what is it that makes this scene so important? Well, it's when *Star Wars* stops being just goodies versus baddies, and becomes something more deliciously scary. Just moments before, we see Lando come good. Now we know good guys can also go bad—and big time!

LIKE FATHER, LIKE SON?

Of course, it's also a vital scene because it raises the specter of Luke turning to the dark side. Vader implores Luke to join with him, so they can rule "as father and son." It adds a personal dimension to the epic space saga, and a whole new dynamic between its most important characters.

SPOILER ALERT!

As with all of Vader's dialogue, the famous "*I am your father*" line was recorded by James Earl Jones after filming. On set, the man playing Vader was David Prowse, who spoke the dialogue prior to dubbing. To stop the big reveal leaking from the set, Prowse was given a different line to say, in this case: "No, Obi-Wan killed your father!" Now, that would have been a very different movie!

THE TRUTH HURTS

Without a weapon, Luke is left helpless on a precipice, but Vader does not finish him. Instead, he says Luke needs to learn what became of his father. Luke says he knows: Vader killed his father. Vader's response is simple yet devastating, "No, I am your father." Though stunning for the audience, it is undeniable for Luke. Deep down, he knows it to be true. He screams, "Noooo!"

QUOTE, UNQUOTE

All pretty memorable, no? Well, up to a point. Read that last section back, and you'll note no one says, "Luke, I am your father." And yet that's how many people remember it. Ah, well. Rick (Humphrey Bogart) never says, "Play it again, Sam," in *Casablanca*, either, so Vader's in good misquoted company.

The scene ends with Luke holding on to a sensor vane for his life.

EPISODE VI:
RETURN OF THE JEDI

"It's a trap!"
ADMIRAL ACKBAR

EPISODE VI: *RETURN OF THE JEDI* AT A GLANCE

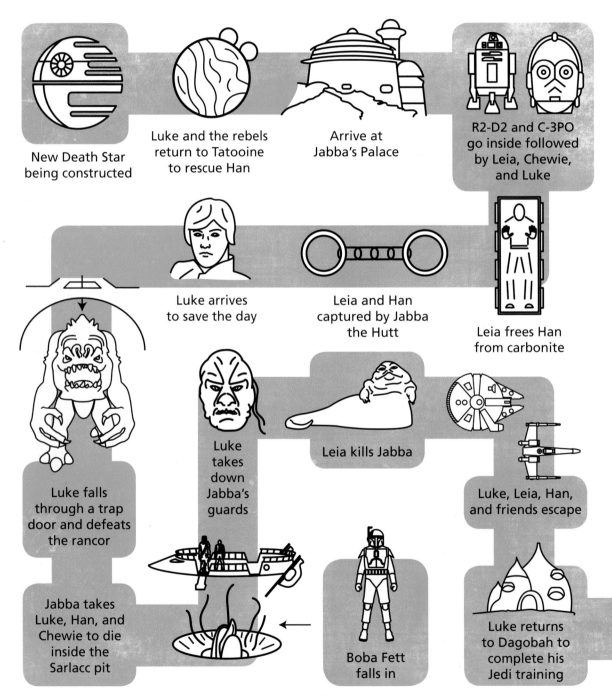

New Death Star being constructed

Luke and the rebels return to Tatooine to rescue Han

Arrive at Jabba's Palace

R2-D2 and C-3PO go inside followed by Leia, Chewie, and Luke

Luke arrives to save the day

Leia and Han captured by Jabba the Hutt

Leia frees Han from carbonite

Luke falls through a trap door and defeats the rancor

Luke takes down Jabba's guards

Leia kills Jabba

Luke, Leia, Han, and friends escape

Jabba takes Luke, Han, and Chewie to die inside the Sarlacc pit

Boba Fett falls in

Luke returns to Dagobah to complete his Jedi training

Rebels plan to attack the second Death Star

...but first need to take down the shield generator

Han pilots stolen shuttle with Luke, Leia, and Chewie

Forest Moon of Endor

Luke and Leia steal speeders to chase troopers

Yoda warns Luke about the dark side, then dies

Rebels and Ewoks fight Imperial troops

Vader takes Luke to see Emperor Palpatine

Luke faces Vader

Leia befriends Ewoks

It's a trap!

Rebel fleet arrives at the second Death Star

Vader kills Palpatine to save Luke

Vader unmasked!

Vader turns back to the light side, then dies

Lando begs Admiral Ackbar to continue the attack to buy time

Battle of Endor

Rebels   vs.   Imperials

Rebels disable Death Star shield generator

Rebels destroy second Death Star

Mon Calamari star cruiser

Second Death Star

Luke cuts off Vader's robotic hand, but refuses to kill him

Ewok party!

Second Death Star blows up Mon Calamari cruiser in the intense space battle

EPISODE VI: *RETURN OF THE JEDI* A CLOSER LOOK

It was the twist that shocked the world: Darth Vader was Luke's father. Was it true? Could Han be rescued? How would it all end? Fans held their breath for three long years to find out.

HOMECOMING

Luke, Leia, R2-D2, and C-3PO return to Tatooine to rescue carbon-frozen Han from Jabba the Hutt. Not too crazy about this plan, Jabba tries to feed Luke to not one, but two monsters. Luke escapes both times.

LEIA THE HUTTSLAYER

Forced into a metal bikini by crime-lord slug Jabba, Leia turns the tables and strangles him with the chain holding her captive. Leia, Han, Luke, and the rest of their friends escape.

When Luke returns to Dagobah for his Jedi training, Yoda confirms Vader is his father and Leia his sister. Then Yoda dies.

EWOKS: FRIENDS OR FOES?

Luke, Han, and Leia meet the Ewoks on Endor. The Ewoks initially want to eat them, but Luke dazzles them with the Force, and they agree to help attack the shield generator protecting the Empire's new Death Star.

LUKE MEETS EMPEROR PALPATINE

Luke tells Leia that—shocker!—they are brother and sister. He then leaves to go meet Vader. He tries to bring him back to the light side of the Force.

> **"I know there is good in you."** *LUKE SKYWALKER*

Instead, Vader brings Luke to the Emperor, who wants to turn him to the dark side.

"IT'S A TRAP!"

Lando and the rebel fleet attack the Death Star above Endor, but the shield is still up and the whole Imperial fleet awaits—plus, the Death Star's superlaser is active!

The Ewoks prove fierce little bears and help blow up the Death Star's shield generator.

LUKE WILL NOT FIGHT

Luke duels Vader to the Emperor's delight, then realizes the only way to defeat the dark side is to follow the path of peace. He throws aside his lightsaber.

> **"I'll never turn to the dark side."** *LUKE SKYWALKER*

ONE WITH THE FORCE

Angered by Luke's pacifism, the Emperor zaps him with Force lightning. Vader steps in to save his son and kills his boss, sacrificing himself and returning to the light side of the Force. The rebels blow up the new Death Star, and Luke sees his dad as a Force ghost in Jedi robes, alongside Yoda and Obi-Wan Kenobi.

GOOD GUYS

LUKE SKYWALKER
The last Jedi,
family problems

HAN SOLO
Carbon-thawed
rebel general

LEIA ORGANA
Rebel leader,
commando

LANDO CALRISSIAN
Falcon pilot,
Death Star destroyer

BAD GUYS

DARTH VADER
Bad dad
come good

BOBA FETT
Bounty hunter,
Sarlacc snack

EMPEROR PALPATINE
Dark side
recruiter

JABBA THE HUTT
Gangster slug, floor
show enthusiast

THE GREAT EWOK DEBATE

They look like teddy bears, love to eat biscuits, and are the only beings alive who appreciate C-3PO's storytelling. But they also want to eat our heroes. Are they kid-friendly or killers?

LOVE 'EM

Small but mighty, the Ewoks are the ultimate expression of *Star Wars*' standout message: the little guy can make a difference even against overwhelming odds. And, just as Luke's pacifism ends the Sith cycle of violence, the Ewoks' back-to-nature ways help to put an end to the Empire's technological terror.

George Lucas was keen to show the Empire could be vulnerable to primitive forces, and originally planned to use the Wookiees. Ewoks are just Wookiees with the syllables swapped over, and no one hates Wookiees, do they?

The Ewoks elevate C-3PO to the status of a god, so we know where he stands in this debate.

> ***"I'm afraid our furry friend has gone and done something... rather rash."***
>
> *C-3PO TO HAN SOLO*

On their first meeting, Han was far from keen on the Ewoks—and some of his best friends are fuzzballs!

HATE 'EM

After three movies where the massed ranks of the Rebel Alliance couldn't bring down the Empire, we're supposed to believe all it takes is help from some *teddy bears*? And who roots for a species that would happily cook and eat our heroes, given half a chance?

Most critics of the Ewoks says they're either too cuddly or too barbaric. But what if their strength comes from being both? Characters such as Han and Vader are lauded for their contradictions, so why not the Ewoks as well?

ANSWER IN A NUTSHELL

Sure, they're savage and slightly silly all at once, but that's not a bad summing-up of the whole, mad, brilliant *Star Wars* universe. So, you've gotta love an Ewok!

Luke calls himself a Jedi, but he never finished his training, so...

IS LUKE A JEDI NOW?

Last time I saw him, Luke got his butt kicked by Daddy Vader. Now he's the Man in Black, sweeping into Jabba's palace and calling himself a Jedi Knight!

WHEN DID LUKE GET SO BADASS?

A year has passed since Luke lost a hand and learned that Darth Vader is his dad. Since then he's realized that he needs to exercise greater control over the Force and his emotions—both to defeat Vader, and to avoid ending up like him. The Luke we meet here has honed his powers, and learned to keep his cool.

HAS HE COMPLETED HIS TRAINING WITH YODA?

Not yet, but he has found time to make himself a brand new lightsaber, an important ritual for any Jedi. When he does return to Dagobah to complete his training, Yoda says he has nothing more to teach him.

SO HE IS A JEDI?

No. Luke does call himself a Jedi Knight when he goes to Jabba's palace, but it is not until later that he truly becomes one by renouncing the dark side, even though it will likely cost him his life.

SO HE COULD STILL TURN TO THE DARK SIDE?

At this point, yeah. This is the darkest we've ever seen Luke—not just in his choice of outfit but in his use of Force chokes and threats of destruction. He may be cool, but he's not yet fully in control...

LUKE SKYWALKER

Since Episode IV, Luke has gone from wearing white, through midtones, to black—an outward expression of the growing darkness within him.

Luke finally realizes what it means to be a Jedi when he refuses to kill Darth Vader in anger—even if it means sacrificing his own life.

> **"Jabba, this is your last chance. Free us, or die."**
> *LUKE SKYWALKER TO JABBA THE HUTT*

George Lucas took the opportunity to make Luke's new lightsaber green instead of blue because he knew it would stand out better against the sky in the scenes set on Tatooine.

WHO IS JABBA THE HUTT?

Sure, I know he's an ugly repellent slug guy, and he's definitely not a goodie, but he doesn't seem to be in the Empire, either. And what is a Hutt, anyway?

IS HE WITH THE EMPIRE?

No—Jabba the Hutt is very much his own slug and wouldn't be a good fit with Imperial discipline (plus an even worse fit through Imperial doors). Instead, he runs his own crime ring, which the Empire tolerates in exchange for Jabba supplying some valuable goods and services—such as bounty hunters.

IS HE A BIG DEAL?

Massive! Beyond his literal size—he is almost 13 ft (4 m) long—he is one of the most powerful figures on Tatooine, running most of the piracy, slavery, and other black market activities that make the planet such a hotbed of scum and villainy. His network of smugglers is extensive, and led to a long and profitable relationship with one Han Solo.

Pah. Manga wanjee kohkpah. *

*Translation:
"There will be
no bargain."

JABBA THE HUTT

SO WHY DOES HE HATE HAN SO MUCH?

Cast your mind back to Episode IV and you'll remember that Han owed Jabba money after the *Millennium Falcon* was forced to ditch a cargo it was carrying on Jabba's behalf.

SO THAT'S WHERE I'VE SEEN HIM BEFORE?

Probably. Jabba appears in a single scene in Episode IV, which was introduced for the Special Edition in 1997. Interestingly, it's a scene that was filmed in the 1970s with Jabba as a human. For the Special Edition, the Jabba we know and "love" was digitally added over the top.

WHO'S WHO IN JABBA'S ENTOURAGE?

The guy with two big tentacles coming out of his head is Bib Fortuna, Jabba's chief of staff. The beaky creature is jester Salacious B. Crumb. Max Rebo is the blue elephant-like band leader, who performs with singer Sy Snootles, and Oola is the green-skinned dancer, with head tentacles of her own.

SO IS "HUTT" JABBA'S NAME OR HIS TITLE?

It's his species, but it gets bandied around because it identifies him as a member of the deadly Hutt Clan crime cartel, too. It's also a heck of a lot easier than saying his full name, which is Jabba Desilijic Tiure!

Jabba keeps a pet rancor beneath his palace, and sends his enemies to meet it via a trapdoor.

Jabba's entourage is made up of many species, including Twi'leks and Kowakian monkey-lizards.

Slimy Jabba dies at the hands of Princess Leia after he tries to kill our heroes Luke, Han, and Chewie.

BATTLE OF ENDOR
MADE SIMPLE

This is it, the final showdown in the Galactic Civil War. The battle between the Rebel Alliance and the Empire is not one to forget.

INFO BOX:
SPACE BATTLE

LOCATION—In space, above the Forest Moon of Endor

KEY BATTLE ZONE—Main reactor of the second Death Star

FORCES—Rebel Alliance and Galactic Empire

REBELS

MILLENNIUM FALCON

B-WINGS

X-WINGS

Y-WINGS

A-WINGS

WHO'S FIGHTING WHO?
The Rebel Alliance is launching a full-scale assault on the Empire in a bid to end the war once and for all. The rebels receive some unexpected help from the Ewoks.

WHY ARE THEY FIGHTING?
The rebels plan to take down the shield generator and destroy the second Death Star while it's still in its vulnerable construction phase.

MON CALAMARI CRUISER

EMPIRE

SUPER STAR DESTROYER

STAR DESTROYERS

TIE FIGHTERS

DEATH STAR II

TIE INTERCEPTORS

TIE FIGHTERS

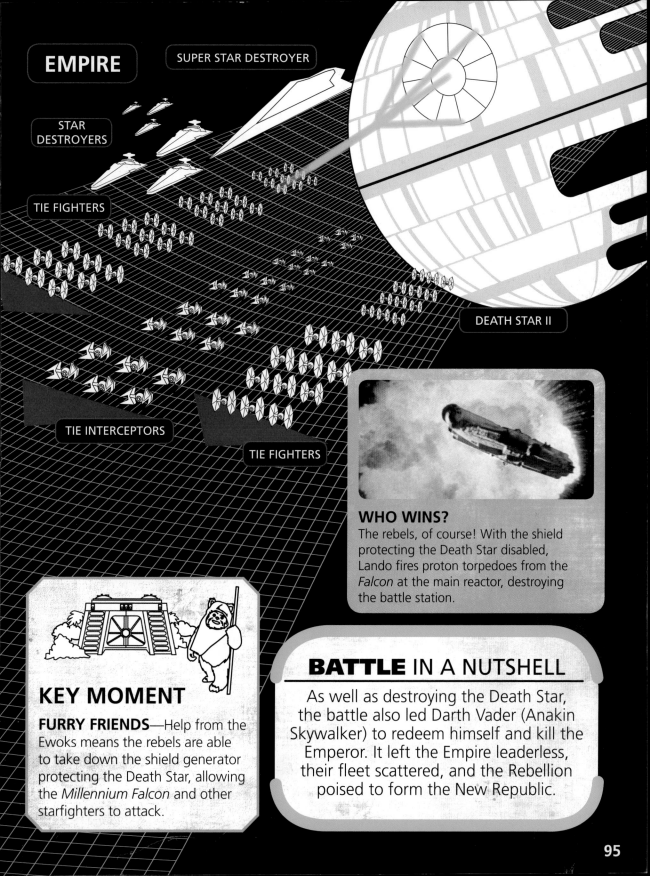

WHO WINS?

The rebels, of course! With the shield protecting the Death Star disabled, Lando fires proton torpedoes from the *Falcon* at the main reactor, destroying the battle station.

KEY MOMENT

FURRY FRIENDS—Help from the Ewoks means the rebels are able to take down the shield generator protecting the Death Star, allowing the *Millennium Falcon* and other starfighters to attack.

BATTLE IN A NUTSHELL

As well as destroying the Death Star, the battle also led Darth Vader (Anakin Skywalker) to redeem himself and kill the Emperor. It left the Empire leaderless, their fleet scattered, and the Rebellion poised to form the New Republic.

You've gotta be kidding me. After all that effort...

THERE'S ANOTHER DEATH STAR?

I definitely saw the Death Star blow up. It had a fatal flaw, Luke used the Force, people got medals. But why bother if the Empire can just build another one?

HOW MANY OF THESE THINGS ARE THERE?

There's never been more than one at a time—and the one that got destroyed in Episode IV was the first one ever. It took many years to design and build the first Death Star, so destroying it was a major victory for the rebels, regardless of whether another was built or not.

The Death Star will be operational as planned.

HOW LONG DID THIS ONE TAKE TO BUILD?

It's just four years since the first Death Star was destroyed, and it's not certain when the Empire began building this souped-up version of the original. Even so, the second Death Star is still a long way from being finished. Much of its superstructure is clearly missing, and it doesn't have a working hyperdrive.

DOES IT HAVE A FATAL FLAW?

It won't have when it's finished! The old exhaust ports are gone, so the rebels need to attack this Death Star while it is still under construction.

MOFF JERJERROD

SO WHAT'S THE PLAN?

The Death Star is so big that a ship the size of the *Millennium Falcon* can fly right inside the belly of the beast and attack its reactor core. But that'll only work while the exterior is unfinished and the defensive shield is down…

A DEFENSIVE SHIELD?

You betcha. The new Death Star is being built near the moon of Endor, so that it can be protected by an Imperial shield generator there. The generator operates separately from the big, round battle station, and projects an impenetrable energy barrier all around it. Cool, huh?

> ## *"Your friends have failed. Now witness the firepower of this fully armed and operational battle station!"*
>
> EMPEROR PALPATINE

SO THE REBELS NEED TO ATTACK THE GENERATOR?

You got it. Take down the shield, then take down the Death Star. Oh, and take on the massed Imperial starfleet, lying in wait behind Endor. Still, at least this Death Star doesn't yet have a working superlaser. Oh, wait. It does…

The key to taking down the Empire's biggest bauble is destroying the shield generator dish that towers above the Endor treetops.

Having missed all the action on the first Death Star, the Emperor secures a window seat for the sequel, keeping a lookout for Luke.

Even the 12-mile (19-km) long Super Star Destroyer *Executor* is dwarfed by the moon-sized second Death Star!

If she can sense whether or not Luke is OK…

COULD LEIA BE A JEDI?

When the Death Star explodes, Leia says she can "feel" that Luke wasn't in the blast. That sounds like some genuine Jedi mind stuff to me.

DOES LEIA HAVE THE FORCE?

Everybody "has" the Force to some degree: it flows through all living things. But the ability to tap into it is stronger in some people than others. That ability runs in families, and Leia is a Skywalker, so yes, she is strong with the Force.

WHY DOESN'T SHE DO OTHER FORCE STUFF?

Like levitating objects and leaping great distances? Because she's never been trained. Luke couldn't do those things until Yoda showed him how, and it would never have crossed his mind to try. Force sensitivity is very rare, and largely forgotten about since the fall of the Jedi. Plus Leia has only just learned that she's a Skywalker!

BUT SHE IS TELEPATHIC?

She certainly has a mental link to Luke, but it's not something she can control. Her wit and empathy are what make her such a smart cookie, not mind-reading.

COULD LUKE TRAIN HER AS A JEDI?

With Yoda gone, he's pretty much the only person who could. Luke certainly seems to have that in mind when he tells Leia, "You have the power, too. In time you'll learn to use it as I have."

LEIA ORGANA

98

WHY WAS LUKE THE ONE WHO GOT TO BE A JEDI?

Simply because, when Luke and Leia were born, Bail Organa of Alderaan offered to give baby Leia a home. This left Obi-Wan Kenobi to look after Luke on Tatooine. If Bail and his wife Breha had dreamed of adopting a baby boy, Luke and Leia's roles may have been reversed.

> **Luke:** *"The force runs strong in my family. My father has it. I have it. And... my sister has it. Yes, it's you, Leia."*
>
> **Princess Leia:** *"I know. Somehow, I've always known."*
>
> LUKE SKYWALKER TO PRINCESS LEIA, RETURN OF THE JEDI

Luke is saved from certain death on (or rather under) Cloud City when Leia senses him calling out to her through the Force.

Force sensitivity may help Leia in ways she is not even aware of, such as when she pilots a speeder bike with Skywalker-esque speed and skill on Endor.

Though she never becomes a Jedi, Leia's ability to sense disturbances in the Force grows to include events with no direct link to her brother, Luke.

He's been the bad guy for a long time, so...

WHY DOES DARTH VADER TURN GOOD?

I've seen him choke his own men to death for coming out of hyperspace too soon! Now I'm meant to believe there's a good guy under that helmet?

WAS HE A GOOD GUY TO BEGIN WITH?

Yes. We learned in Episode V that Darth Vader is Luke's dad, and we know from Obi-Wan in Episode IV that Luke's dad was a great Jedi before "Darth Vader" killed him. In Episode VI, Obi-Wan's Force ghost clarifies this: Luke's father—Anakin Skywalker—was seduced by the dark side of the Force and became Darth Vader, destroying the man he was before.

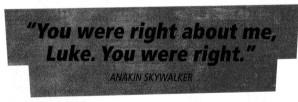

> *"You were right about me, Luke. You were right."*
>
> ANAKIN SKYWALKER

SO GOOD STILL EXISTS WITHIN HIM?

We've seen from his actions that there is no good left within Darth Vader—this is the guy who stood by while the Death Star destroyed a whole planet! But what does remain is the potential for good: some trace of Anakin that just needs to be triggered.

DARTH VADER

SO WHAT TRIGGERS IT?

The last time they met, Vader was more powerful than Luke. Now Luke has the upper hand, and can destroy Vader if he is willing to give in to his anger. But instead, Luke casts aside his weapon, realizing that peace is the true path of a Jedi. In that moment, Vader sees the choice he could have made many years before, and understands—for the very first time—that there is another way.

DOES THAT MAKE UP FOR ALL THE BAD STUFF?

No, and Vader knows it. He can never again walk the path of peace, but he can help his son to do so. Using his talent for violence one last time, he turns on the Emperor and sacrifices himself to destroy Palpatine. For a moment before he dies, he is Anakin again, and his Force ghost endures thereafter. The great Jedi Anakin Skywalker has finally killed Darth Vader.

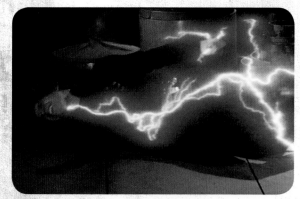

Luke's willingness to sacrifice himself rather than turn to the dark side inspires Vader, just as Luke was once inspired by Obi-Wan's sacrifice.

Vader takes on the Emperor to save his son, but also to save the man he once was. Most of all, he does it because he knows it's right.

Vader—or rather, Anakin—knows he is dying, so asks Luke to remove his life-support mask, in order to look on his son with his human eyes.

As the rebels and the Ewoks celebrate the end of the Empire, Luke sees his father's Force ghost standing alongside those of Yoda and Obi-Wan.

EPISODE I:
THE PHANTOM MENACE

"I will come back and free you, Mom. I promise."

ANAKIN SKYWALKER

EPISODE I: *THE PHANTOM MENACE* AT A GLANCE

Trade Federation
blockades Naboo

Jedi Qui-Gon and
apprentice Obi-Wan
arrive at blockade

Darth Sidious orders
Jedi killed

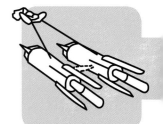

Anakin
enters
Podrace
to help
Jedi

Jedi meet
native Gungan
Jar Jar Binks

Trade
Federation
invades
Naboo

Jedi escape
to Naboo

Jedi and
Jar Jar
face sea
monsters

Stop-off for
repairs on
Tatooine

They
have no
funds to
buy spare
parts

Sidious sends
Darth Maul
to attack Jedi

They rescue Queen
Amidala from
Trade Federation

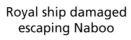

Royal ship damaged
escaping Naboo

They meet slave boy
Anakin Skywalker

Jedi escape Darth Maul with Anakin

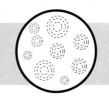

Coruscant—home of Jedi Council and Galactic Senate

Yoda refuses to train Anakin

Anakin wins funds, and his freedom

Amidala gets Gungan leader to help

Jedi, Jar Jar, Anakin, and Amidala return to Naboo

Senate rejects plea to help Naboo

Battle of Naboo

vs.

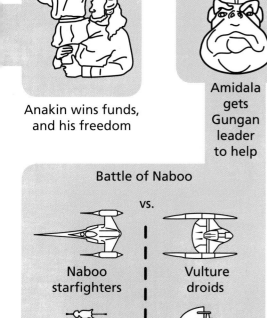

Naboo starfighters

Vulture droids

Fambaas

Armored Assault Tanks (AATs)

Trade Federation droid army shuts down

Yoda lets Obi-Wan train Anakin

Anakin destroys droid control ship

Darth Maul kills Qui-Gon

Obi-Wan cuts Darth Maul in half

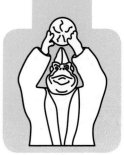

Naboo street party!

EPISODE I: *THE PHANTOM MENACE* A CLOSER LOOK

Sixteen years after the release of Return of the Jedi *came the first of three prequels. Fans couldn't wait to see how the Skywalker saga began and to find out how Luke's dad Anakin became Darth Vader.* The Phantom Menace *started to fill in the gaps.*

GALACTIC GRIEVANCES

Thirty-two years before the events of *A New Hope*, Jedi Qui-Gon Jinn and his apprentice Obi-Wan Kenobi try to resolve the Trade Federation's blockade of peaceful planet Naboo. But all-round bad guy Darth Sidious orders them killed.

"Kill them immediately." SIDIOUS

A Naboo native, the bumbling Gungan Jar Jar Binks helps the Jedi escape the Trade Federation and rescue Naboo's Queen Amidala. Droid R2-D2 saves their ship as they blast through the blockade, but it's left badly damaged.

Padmé lands on Tatooine and meets slave boy Anakin. He is smitten with her and calls her an angel.

PODRACING

The ship is forced to land on Tatooine, in need of expensive repairs. Padmé meets young Anakin, who offers to enter a deadly podrace to win the funds they need. Qui-Gon bargains for Anakin's freedom if he wins. And guess what—Anakin comes in first!

GETTING MAULED

Turns out Anakin's really strong with the Force, so he leaves his beloved mom to train with Qui-Gon as a Jedi. Before they take off, Sidious' apprentice, Darth Maul, attacks but fails to kill them. The group heads to Coruscant so Padmé can request help from the Galactic Senate to fight the corrupt Trade Federation.

CHILLY RECEPTION

The Jedi Council refuses to train Anakin as they feel he is too old. The Senate also refuses to move against the Trade Federation, so Naboo's senator, Palpatine, bids to become leader of the Senate.

GUNGANS TO THE RESCUE

Padmé, the Jedi, and Anakin return to Naboo and enlist the help of the Gungans to repel the Trade Federation. All-out battle ensues.

Darth Maul kills Qui-Gon, and Obi-Wan returns the favor by cutting Maul in half.

SKYWALKER SHINES

Anakin blows up the ship controlling the Trade Federation's droid army, winning the day. Yoda agrees to let Obi-Wan train the boy, in whom the newly elected Chancellor Palpatine also shows great interest. The identity of Darth Maul's master remains a mystery the Jedi will have to solve…

GOOD GUYS

QUI-GON JINN
Rebellious Jedi,
Obi-Wan's teacher

OBI-WAN KENOBI
Padawan who
becomes a Knight

ANAKIN SKYWALKER
Slave, podracer,
mama's boy

PADMÉ AMIDALA
Queen of Naboo

JAR JAR BINKS
Bumbling but
loyal Gungan

BOSS NASS
Gungan leader,
phlegmy

BAD GUYS

DARTH SIDIOUS
Sith Lord,
hood-wearer

DARTH MAUL
Sith apprentice,
tattoo aficionado

Some people seem to love him, so why is there still…

THE GREAT JAR JAR BINKS DIVIDE

His heart's in the right place and he helps bring the Gungans into the battle to save Naboo. So why do some people think Jar Jar should have been canned?

IS IT BECAUSE HE'S FUNNY?

Well, Jar Jar was intended to bring the laughs in the prequel trilogy—a vital role in an otherwise difficult story about Anakin's fall to the dark side. Trouble is, some fans wanted nothing but the darkness, having waited so long to find out about it, and they weren't willing to suffer Jar Jar gladly.

IS IT BECAUSE HE'S SUCH AN UNLIKELY HERO?

In a way. Even though *Star Wars* is all about unlikely heroes, Jar Jar's rise from goofball to Gungan general sat uncomfortably with some fans. They could cope with him being one or the other, but not both.

> **"Wesa got a grand army. That's why you no liking us, mesa thinks."** *JAR JAR BINKS*

JAR JAR BINKS

IS IT THOSE DELIGHTFUL FLOPPY EARS?

Funny you ask, because in 1999 those ears were one of the things that made Jar Jar the most advanced computer-generated movie character ever. Even if you don't like him, you've got to admire the workmanship that paved the way for big-screen characters such as Gollum and the Hulk, not to mention Maz Kanata in Episode VII: *The Force Awakens*.

IS IT WRONG FOR ME TO LIKE HIM?

Actually, no. Since *The Phantom Menace* was released in 1999, fans have come to see that *Star Wars* is a vast universe that can be many things to many people. Also, loads of kids loved Jar Jar from the start, and never cared that he isn't wrestling with heavy issues.

Qui-Gon Jinn saves Jar Jar's life the first time he appears in *The Phantom Menace*. Some *Star Wars* fans never forgave him for this.

Like the droids in the original trilogy, Jar Jar allow audiences to see the story from the point of view of a secondary character.

For the climax of Episode I, Jar Jar is promoted to Bombad General in the Gungan Army. By Episode II he is acting as a Galactic Senator!

He may be divisive in real life, but in the movie Jar Jar helps unite the two sentient species on Naboo, as seen in the closing celebration.

I thought Star Wars was all about action and adventure, so…

WHAT'S WITH ALL THE POLITICS?

Turmoil in the Galactic Republic! Taxes on trade routes! Endless debates in the Senate! The opening crawl of Episode I makes me think I should have paid more attention in civics class…

WHAT IS THE GALACTIC SENATE?

The governing body of the Republic that rules the galaxy, the Senate is an assembly of elected representatives from hundreds of member worlds and business guilds. It was formed with noble, democratic ideals, but bribery and self-interest has corrupted it.

> **"The Republic is not what it once was."**
> SENATOR PALPATINE

BUSINESSES GET THEIR OWN SENATORS?

Yup. Much like the East India Company on Earth in the 19th century, groups like the Trade Federation wield great power, and act more like independent states than businesses. The Trade Federation is ruled by a viceroy and even has its own battleships and armies.

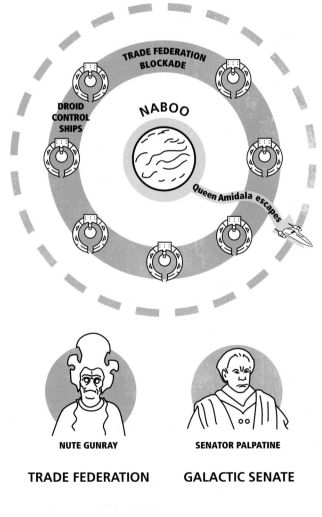

TRADE FEDERATION BLOCKADE

DROID CONTROL SHIPS

NABOO

Queen Amidala escapes

NUTE GUNRAY

TRADE FEDERATION

SENATOR PALPATINE

GALACTIC SENATE

IS THAT A GOOD IDEA?

No, not really. When the Trade Federation decides it doesn't want to pay its taxes, it brings out the big guns and blockades the trade routes to the planet Naboo.

AND SO THE SENATE DOES… WHAT?

Nothing. No one wants to rock the boat, so poor old Naboo gets cut off from the rest of the galaxy.

DOESN'T NABOO HAVE ITS OWN SENATORS?

Funny you should ask. In response to the Senate's inaction, Naboo's Senator Palpatine pushes for its leader, Chancellor Valorum, to be replaced. And it just so happens the prime candidate to take over is… Naboo's Senator Palpatine.

IS THAT A PROBLEM?

It would be pretty standard political maneuvering if it wasn't for one thing: Palpatine is secretly responsible for the blockade of Naboo in the first place! As his alter ego, Darth Sidious, he has conspired with the Trade Federation leadership to engineer a crisis, precisely so he can seize power in the Senate.

SO POLITICS *IS* EXCITING!

It is if you're a Sith Lord—and that, though nobody knows it yet, is exactly what Palpatine is. Becoming Chancellor is his first step to making himself Emperor.

The Trade Federation is led by Neimoidian Nute Gunray, who allows himself to be manipulated by Darth Sidious—a.k.a. Senator Palpatine.

Senator Palpatine encourages Queen Amidala of Naboo to address the Senate, calling for a vote of no confidence in his rival, Chancellor Valorum.

Galactic Senators gather for votes and debates in a vast, circular chamber lined with more than a thousand hovering repulsorpod platforms.

I don't really follow sports, so...

WHAT'S THE DEAL WITH PODRACING?

When I heard we were getting the backstory of Darth Vader, I never guessed he'd be in a helmet so soon—or that he would look so cute in one!

WHAT IS PODRACING?

Podracing is an extreme sport popular on the planet Tatooine. Competitors ride in small chariots pulled by oversized engines, racing through a mountainous dirt route at terrifying speeds.

WHY IS IT IMPORTANT?

Gambling on podraces is rife on Tatooine. When Qui-Gon and Padmé need parts for their ship, they have no choice but to wager for them. Luckily, they have a secret weapon in the shape of young Anakin Skywalker, who has Jedi reflexes and a pod of his own.

HOW DOES A SLAVE BOY HAVE HIS OWN POD?

Anakin is the property of junk dealer and podracing enthusiast Watto. Watto lets the boy race and acquire the parts he needs because Watto can make money by gambling against him. And if he crashes or gets shot by Tusken Raiders in the process… well, he's only a slave.

> **"Sebulba's in the lead, followed closely by Skywalker!"**
> COMMENTATOR BEED

WHY ARE PEOPLE SHOOTING AT THEM?

Tatooine is a lawless world, and podracing a lawless sport. Tusken Raiders will claim anything they can get their hands on in the desert—even if they have to shoot it first. A bigger risk for most podracers is falling foul of the dirty tricks practiced by fellow racers. Bookies' favorite Sebulba, for example, has become a champion by using a flamethrower on his opponents.

ANAKIN'S PODRACER

Anakin's Force connection means he can sense things before they happen, making him the only human with reflexes fast enough for podracing.

PODRACERS

ANAKIN SKYWALKER
Has yet to finish a podrace

SEBULBA
Cheating champ who usually gets away with it

GASGANO
Four arms give him complete control

BEN QUADINAROS
Gets stuck on the starting grid

RATTS
Tiny guy with big engines and a bigger wipeout

MARS GUO
His pod blows up, thanks to Sebulba

BAD GUYS

JABBA
Odious MC of the Boonta Eve Classic podrace

WATTO
Junk dealer with a gambling problem

113

WHO IS PADMÉ?

She's the teen Queen of Naboo who seems to wear something different in every scene. But who's the young woman behind the wardrobe?

WHY IS THERE A QUEEN IN THE REPUBLIC?

Padmé Amidala is the Queen of the planet Naboo, one of the thousands of worlds that make up the Galactic Republic. Every one of those worlds has its own independent system of government, and Padmé was elected to be Naboo's head of state when she was just 14.

BUT YOU DON'T VOTE FOR QUEENS!

They do on Naboo! Rather than having royal blood, Padmé won her position by dedicating her childhood to public service. She may be young, but she has many experienced advisors to call on, such as Naboo's representative on the Galactic Senate, Senator Palpatine.

GOOD MAN, IS HE?

Um… well, he's certainly one of Padmé's most trusted aides. Palpatine counsels her after the Trade Federation invades Naboo, convincing her that the only way to save her people is to ask the Senate for a vote of no confidence in its ineffectual leader, Chancellor Valorum.

PADMÉ AMIDALA

DOES THAT HELP?

It mostly just helps Palpatine's political career. So Padmé sets out to save Naboo herself, negotiating an alliance with its native Gungans and taking up arms alongside her own Royal Guard to defeat the Trade Federation.

WHY DOES PADMÉ GO UNDERCOVER?

With many enemies out to get her, the Queen has her handmaiden Sabé take her place as a decoy to offer her protection. Sabé was played by a pre-fame Keira Knightley.

A WARDROBE FIT FOR A QUEEN

FOR ADDRESSING THE SENATE

FOR MEETING DIGNITARIES

FOR THE THRONE ROOM

FOR GOING UNDERCOVER

FOR PARADES

FOR TRAVEL

FOR BATTLE

FOR INFORMAL RECEPTIONS

WHO IS DARTH MAUL?

So I've seen this guy with a horny head and some hardcore tattoos, and I'm guessing he's not one of the goodies.

IS DARTH MAUL NAMED AFTER DARTH VADER?

No, we've gone back in time for Episode I, so there is no Darth Vader yet! "Darth" isn't Maul's name—and it's not Vader's either. It's a title used by Sith Lords. For example, before he becomes the Emperor, Palpatine also goes by the name Darth Sidious.

SO HE'S A NEW SITH LORD?

New to us, yes. But Darth Sidious has been training him since childhood to be a rage-filled, Jedi-hating warrior who will do his dirty work for him. As Sidious' apprentice, Maul has been brought up to believe Sidious is the rightful ruler of the galaxy.

DARTH SIDIOUS IS AROUND IN THIS ERA, TOO?

Yes, but he's a long way from becoming Emperor. At this point in time, the Sith are believed to be long extinct, and both Sidious and Maul have gone to great lengths to hide their existence from the Sith's ancient enemies, the Jedi.

DARTH MAUL

DARTH MAUL IS IN HIDING?

Well, he was, but then the Jedi freed Queen Amidala from the blockaded planet Naboo. That jeopardizes Sidious' plans, so Maul has to move against the Jedi to get the Queen back. Maul's confident he will kill Qui-Gon, though, so it's not as if he's about to reveal the Sith to the whole Jedi Order for the first time in a thousand years… Unfortunately for Maul, Qui-Gon gets away in the Queen's ship.

HOW DOES QUI-GON KNOW MAUL IS A SITH?

Only a Sith Lord fights with Darth Maul's combination of Jedi skills and total anger. His cool, red, double-bladed lightsaber is a bit of a giveaway, too.

SO NOT THE TATTOOS?

No—Maul is Zabrak, not human, and was born into a tribe known as the Nightbrothers on the planet Dathomir. Had Qui-Gon recognized the tattoos, he would have known they were common to the Nightbrothers, not the Sith.

WHAT ABOUT HIS HORNS?

Also standard for Zabraks. Interestingly though, the concept art for the character originally showed them as feathers. When George Lucas saw the design, he mistook them for horns—and liked them!

Though it looks cool, Maul's double-bladed lightsaber requires a special fighting technique, rarely used by Sith or Jedi.

Maul kills Qui-Gon Jinn, only to be sliced in two by Qui-Gon's lightsaber—wielded by the late Jedi's Padawan, Obi-Wan Kenobi.

Maul survives his bisection to appear in *Star Wars: The Clone Wars* and *Star Wars Rebels* on TV, modeling different sets of cybernetic legs.

BATTLE OF NABOO MADE SIMPLE

With seemingly only the destiny of one planet at stake, no one could have predicted how the result of this battle would change the Republic forever.

GUNGAN GRAND ARMY

FAMBAA SHIELD GENERATOR MOUNTS

BOOMA CATAPULTS

WHO'S FIGHTING WHO?

The Gungan Grand Army intend to lure Trade Federation forces away from the human capital, Theed, to the Great Grass Plains, allowing Queen Amidala to infiltrate the city and capture Trade Federation Viceroy, Nute Gunray. Starfighters will destroy the Federation Droid Control Ship.

INFO BOX

LOCATION—The Great Grass Plains of Naboo

TERRAIN—Idyllic green grasslands

FORCES—Gungan Grand Army and Trade Federation forces

WHY ARE THEY FIGHTING?

Trade Federation forces have invaded Naboo and taken control. After the Galactic Senate refuses to help, Queen Amidala plans the attack to liberate her home planet.

MTTs

AATs

DROIDEKAS

B1 BATTLE DROIDS

GUNGANS

KAADU MOUNTS

SHIELD ZONE

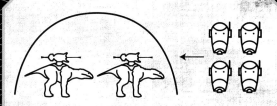

KEY MOMENT

SHIELDS DOWN—The Gungan shields hold firm against the Federation's AATs, but when the battle droids are deployed, they penetrate the shields. The Grand Army is defeated, and it doesn't look good for Naboo.

WHO WINS?

Anakin Skywalker destroys the Droid Control Ship, shutting down the droid army on Naboo's surface. With Queen Amidala's capture of Gunray, they appear to have won the battle.

ANSWER IN A NUTSHELL

The Naboo and Gungans forge a new alliance and retake their planet. However, what they don't know is that the battle is actually part of a much larger plan formed by Palpatine in his quest to become Emperor.

EPISODE II:
ATTACK OF THE CLONES

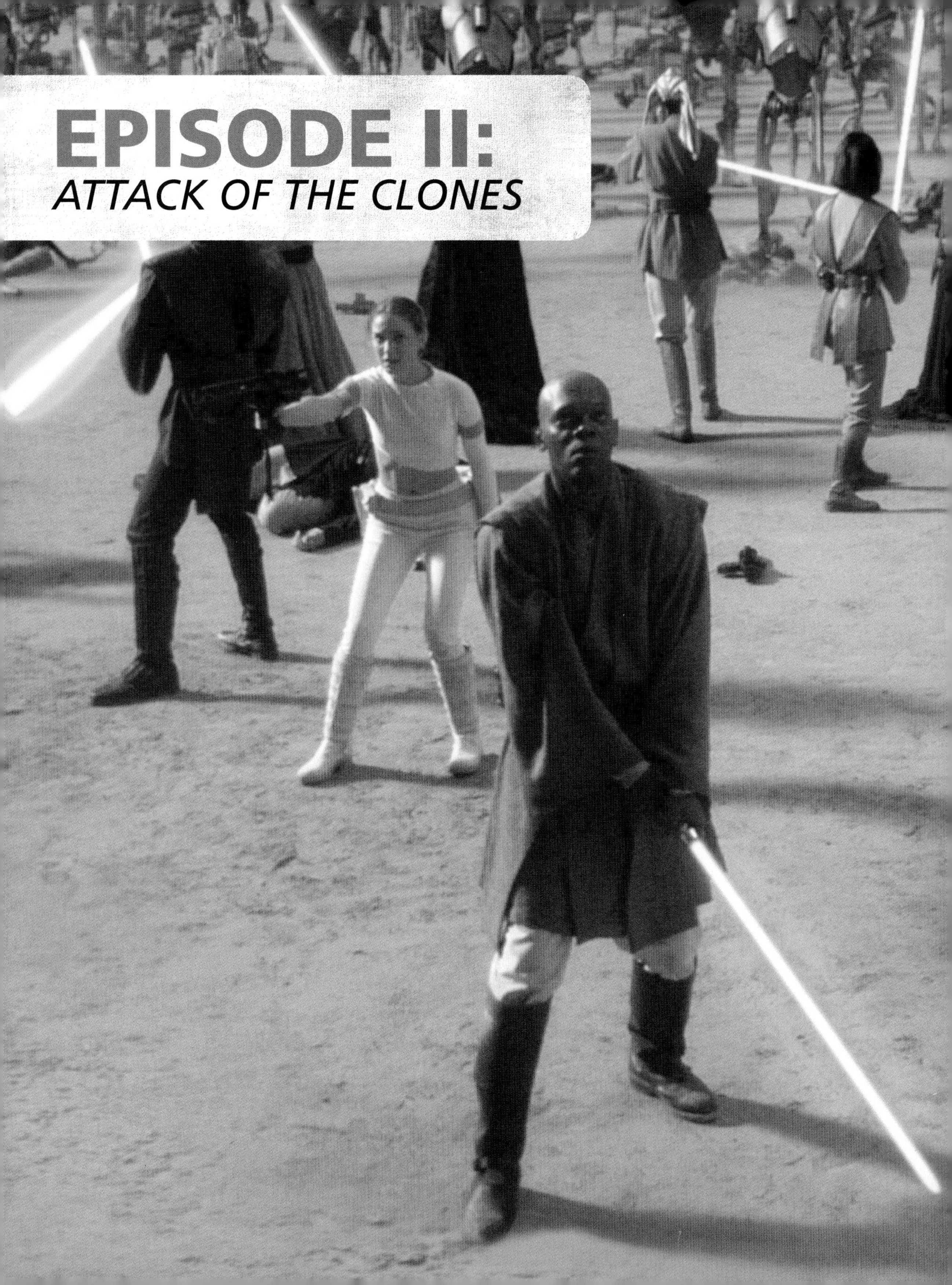

"I truly, deeply love you, and before we die I want you to know."

PADMÉ AMIDALA TO ANAKIN SKYWALKER

EPISODE II: *ATTACK OF THE CLONES* AT A GLANCE

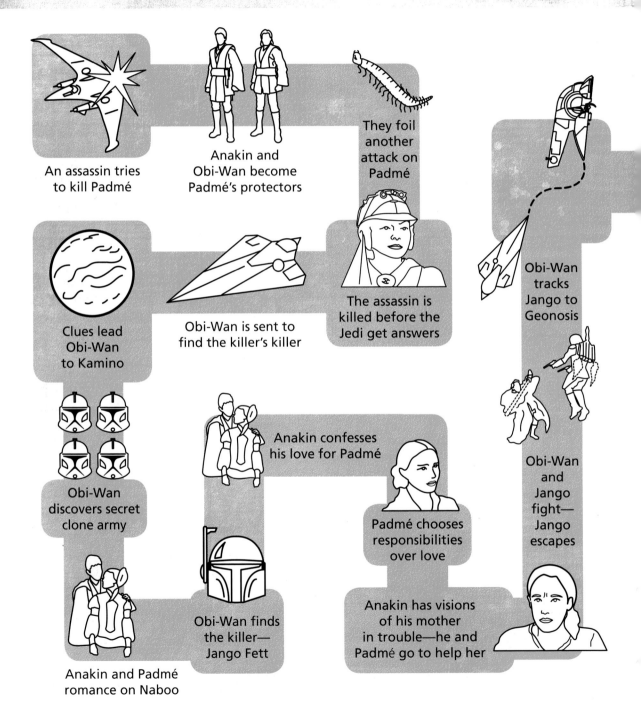

An assassin tries to kill Padmé

Anakin and Obi-Wan become Padmé's protectors

They foil another attack on Padmé

Obi-Wan tracks Jango to Geonosis

Clues lead Obi-Wan to Kamino

Obi-Wan is sent to find the killer's killer

The assassin is killed before the Jedi get answers

Obi-Wan discovers secret clone army

Anakin confesses his love for Padmé

Obi-Wan and Jango fight—Jango escapes

Padmé chooses responsibilities over love

Anakin and Padmé romance on Naboo

Obi-Wan finds the killer—Jango Fett

Anakin has visions of his mother in trouble—he and Padmé go to help her

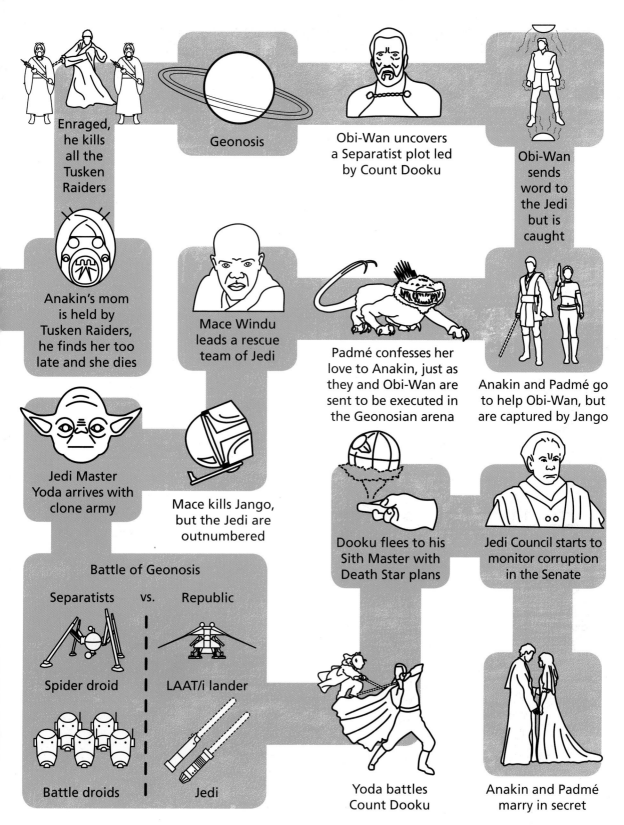

Enraged, he kills all the Tusken Raiders

Geonosis

Obi-Wan uncovers a Separatist plot led by Count Dooku

Obi-Wan sends word to the Jedi but is caught

Anakin's mom is held by Tusken Raiders, he finds her too late and she dies

Mace Windu leads a rescue team of Jedi

Padmé confesses her love to Anakin, just as they and Obi-Wan are sent to be executed in the Geonosian arena

Anakin and Padmé go to help Obi-Wan, but are captured by Jango

Jedi Master Yoda arrives with clone army

Mace kills Jango, but the Jedi are outnumbered

Dooku flees to his Sith Master with Death Star plans

Jedi Council starts to monitor corruption in the Senate

Battle of Geonosis

Separatists   vs.   Republic

Spider droid   LAAT/i lander

Battle droids   Jedi

Yoda battles Count Dooku

Anakin and Padmé marry in secret

123

EPISODE II: *ATTACK OF THE CLONES* A CLOSER LOOK

Set ten years after The Phantom Menace, *Episode II: Attack of the Clones introduces an older, but not necessarily wiser, Anakin Skywalker, and sheds light on the Clone Wars first mentioned by Obi-Wan Kenobi in Episode IV…*

POWDER-KEG POLITICS

Whole solar systems are quitting the Galactic Republic, under the banner of Separatist leader Count Dooku. There is already unrest in the Galactic Senate when an attempt is made on the life of Senator Padmé Amidala.

ANAKIN ENAMORED

Ten years after they last met, trainee Jedi Anakin Skywalker is assigned to guard Padmé. Before long, Anakin falls head over heels in love with her.

The assassin tries a second time to kill Padmé, but that attempt is foiled too. When the assassin is killed, it only raises further questions.

"Do you like your army?"
JANGO FETT TO OBI-WAN KENOBI

THE FETT SET

Anakin's Jedi Master, Obi-Wan Kenobi, goes in search of answers and locates a secret clone army—supposedly made for the Jedi. Each is a clone of shady bounty hunter Jango Fett, whom Obi-Wan pursues to the planet Geonosis.

ANAKIN ENRAGED

Anakin senses that his mother is in danger and goes to her. She is a prisoner of Tusken Raiders, and dies in his arms. Enraged, he not only murders her captors, but also the innocent members of their community.

LOCKED UP IN LOVE

On Geonosis, Obi-Wan learns that the Separatists have a new droid army ready to attack. He gets word to the Jedi, but is then captured. Anakin and Padmé go to rescue him, but are also caught. As they face death, Padmé confesses that she reciprocates Anakin's love for her.

THE JEDI STRIKE BACK

A Jedi strike force arrives and saves Padmé, Anakin, and Obi-Wan from the deadly beasts of the Geonosian arena, but they are no match for an entire droid army. In the nick of time, Jedi Master Yoda appears—leading the secret army of clones.

Yoda duels with Count Dooku, who has become a powerful Sith Lord. Dooku fights dirty, then flees.

CLONE WAR!

Dooku returns to his Sith Master, Darth Sidious, who is pleased that war has broken out between the Republic and the Separatists—just as he planned. As the Clone Wars begin to rage, Anakin goes against the Jedi rules and marries Padmé in a secret ceremony.

GOOD GUYS

ANAKIN SKYWALKER
Padawan with
rage issues

OBI-WAN KENOBI
Jedi turned
detective

PADMÉ AMIDALA
Former queen now
devoted senator

YODA
Jedi Master with
awesome moves

BAD GUYS

COUNT DOOKU
Jedi turned Sith
and Separatist

DARTH SIDIOUS
Pulling the
Separatist strings

JANGO FETT
Face that launched
a million clones

ZAM WESELL
Assassinated
assassin

I'm guessing they're not an art movement, so...

WHO ARE THE SEPARATISTS?

So a bunch of star systems are causing trouble and that leads to the Clone Wars. But who are these bad guys and what's their beef?

WHAT ARE THEY SEPARATE FROM?

The Separatists have broken away from the Galactic Republic. They have formed their own Confederacy of Independent Systems in protest to high taxes levied by the Republic and the corruption within its Senate.

IS THAT UNREASONABLE?

Not really. The Separatists are right that the Senate has become corrupt, and is ineffectual as a result. That much was proved when the Trade Federation was allowed to invade the Republic member world of Naboo.

SO WHAT'S THE PROBLEM?

Only that the Separatists' independence is an illusion. Their leadership and entire manifesto are secretly controlled by the evil Sith Lord Darth Sidious—who also covertly controls the Galactic Senate. Sidious has engineered the Separatist movement from as far back as the invasion of Naboo.

We shall have an army greater than any in the galaxy!

COUNT DOOKU

126

WHY DOESN'T ANYONE REALIZE?

Well, aside from having legitimate points to make, many of the Separatist leaders are greedy businessmen, such as Viceroy Nute Gunray of the Trade Federation. They're worried less about the finer points of ideology behind their movement and more about what they can get out of it. Also, the ultimate head of the Separatists is Count Dooku, a convincing and highly respected former Jedi. He's not going to be involved in anything shady, is he?

WELL IS HE?

Of course he is! He's actually the only one who knows that Sidious is behind it all, having become the Sith Lord's latest apprentice, Darth Tyranus. But even he doesn't realize Sidious' true plan.

AND THAT IS?

Ultimately very unlucky for Dooku, but more immediately: war. If a major conflict threatens the Republic's very existence, its people will demand action in the form of militarization and tough leadership. And Sidious intends to provide both in his guise as Republic Supreme Chancellor Palpatine.

WHAT DOES THAT MEAN FOR THE SEPARATISTS?

In the end, the Separatists are just pawns in Sidious' long game. He will happily see them destroyed to advance his ambitions.

Ten years after its attack on Naboo, Neimoidian Nute Gunray allied the powerful Trade Federation with the Separatist cause.

Geonosian Poggle the Lesser is a leading Separatist who sparked war by sentencing Republic citizens Padmé and Anakin to death.

The Separatists command vast battalions of combat droids, allowing them to seriously challenge the Republic's galactic supremacy.

It seems to be a hot topic in the Galactic Senate…

DOES THE REPUBLIC NEED AN ARMY?

War! What is it good for? Probably quite a lot if your film franchise is called "Star Wars…" So why is this even up for debate?

ISN'T THERE ALREADY A REPUBLIC ARMY?

No. Individual planets may have their own small armed forces, such as the Royal Guard on Naboo, but thanks to 1,000 years of peace, the Republic has never formed an interplanetary army. Or, to put it another way, thanks to never forming an interplanetary army, the Republic has enjoyed 1,000 years of peace.

WHAT ABOUT THE JEDI?

The Jedi Knights are the Republic's peacekeepers and dispute solvers, but they are not soldiers. For all their acrobatic skills and lightsaber smarts, they are sworn to fight only in self-defense. Besides, there are only a few thousand Jedi in total. They are not equipped to fight a war that threatens to rage across many planets at once.

> **"If the Senate votes to create an army, I'm sure it's going to push us into a civil war."**
>
> *SENATOR PADMÉ AMIDALA*

CLONE TROOPER

WHAT'S THE CASE FOR HAVING AN ARMY NOW?

The rise of the Separatist movement has caused thousands of star systems to break away from the Republic and form a large Confederacy of Independent Systems. So, for the first time in a millennium, there are two major power blocs in the galaxy. That raises the possibility of conflict, in theory—and in practice the Confederacy is known to be capable of deploying vast droid armies, just as the Separatist Trade Federation did when it invaded Naboo.

AND WHAT'S THE ARGUMENT AGAINST?

If one thing is guaranteed to start a war, it's spooking the Separatists by preparing for one. This is the argument put forward in the Senate by Padmé Amidala, who has been elected as a senator after fulfilling her term as Queen of Naboo.

WHO'S RIGHT?

It's complicated. In the long run, no good comes from having a Grand Army of the Republic, but not having one wouldn't have helped much, either. The trouble is, Darth Sidious is secretly controlling both the Republic and the Separatists so, war or no war, he's going to come out on top. The Separatists do eventually start a war, and had they been unopposed, events would probably have played out in much the same way as they already do in Episode III, only sooner.

When Darth Sidious learns that a Jedi called Sifo-Dyas has secretly commissioned a clone army, he incorporates it into his plans.

The Senate debates a Military Creation Act to legally permit the Republic to make use of the clone army, but no vote is forthcoming.

When the Senate votes to give the Chancellor emergency powers, no further debate is needed, and the clone army is legitimized.

BATTLE OF GEONOSIS
MADE SIMPLE

A dusty desert world populated by the insect-like Geonosians is the site of a battle that will change the course of history for many years to come.

INFO BOX

LOCATION—Planet of Geonosis

TERRAIN—Arid plains around rocky outcroppings containing droid factories

FORCES—Grand Army of the Republic and Confederacy of Independent Systems forces

REPUBLIC

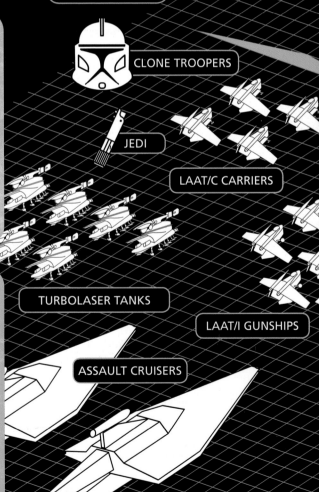

CLONE TROOPERS

JEDI

LAAT/C CARRIERS

TURBOLASER TANKS

LAAT/I GUNSHIPS

ASSAULT CRUISERS

WHO'S FIGHTING WHO?
The Republic forces, Jedi, and the newly discovered army of clone troopers take on the Confederacy of Independent Systems (Separatist) forces.

WHY ARE THEY FIGHTING?
When the Republic discovers the Separatists are amassing an army of battle droids, vehicles, and weaponry on Geonosis, it must act. The Republic invades Geonosis and engages the droid army in battle.

SEPARATISTS

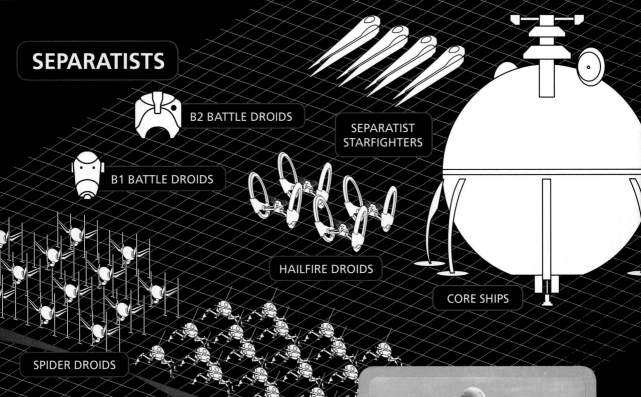

B2 BATTLE DROIDS

B1 BATTLE DROIDS

SEPARATIST STARFIGHTERS

HAILFIRE DROIDS

CORE SHIPS

SPIDER DROIDS

DWARF SPIDER DROIDS

WHO WINS?

There is no clear winner of this battle. The Republic suffers heavy losses, including many Jedi, while Count Dooku and other Separatist leaders escape from Geonosis.

KEY MOMENT

BATTLE ARENA—Yoda and the clone army rescue Anakin, Padmé, Obi-Wan, and a group of Jedi from execution in a gladiator-style arena at the start of the battle.

BATTLE IN A NUTSHELL

Without a decisive victory for the Republic, the battle marks the beginning of the Clone Wars—three years of fighting and struggle for power.

131

EPISODE III:
REVENGE OF THE SITH

"You have allowed this Dark Lord to twist your mind..."

OBI-WAN KENOBI TO DARTH VADER

EPISODE III: *REVENGE OF THE SITH* AT A GLANCE

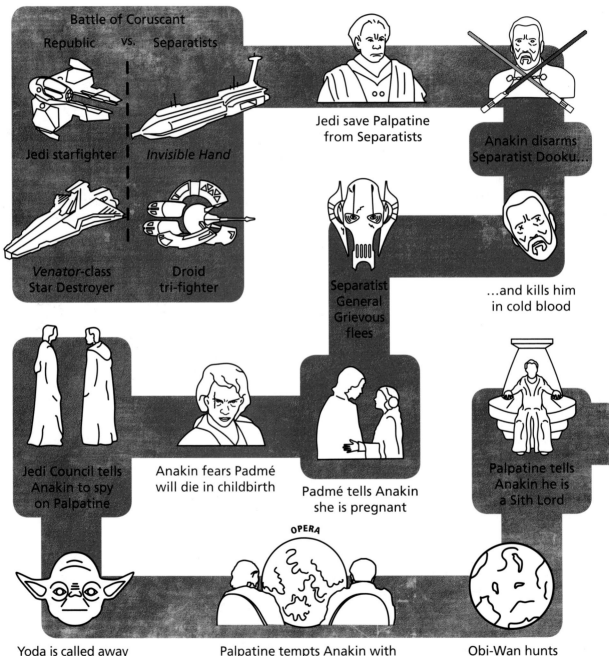

Battle of Coruscant

Republic vs. Separatists

Jedi starfighter | *Invisible Hand*

Venator-class Star Destroyer | Droid tri-fighter

Jedi save Palpatine from Separatists

Anakin disarms Separatist Dooku...

...and kills him in cold blood

Separatist General Grievous flees

Jedi Council tells Anakin to spy on Palpatine

Anakin fears Padmé will die in childbirth

Padmé tells Anakin she is pregnant

Palpatine tells Anakin he is a Sith Lord

OPERA

Yoda is called away to fight on Kashyyyk

Palpatine tempts Anakin with Sith secrets to hold back death

Obi-Wan hunts Grievous on Utapau

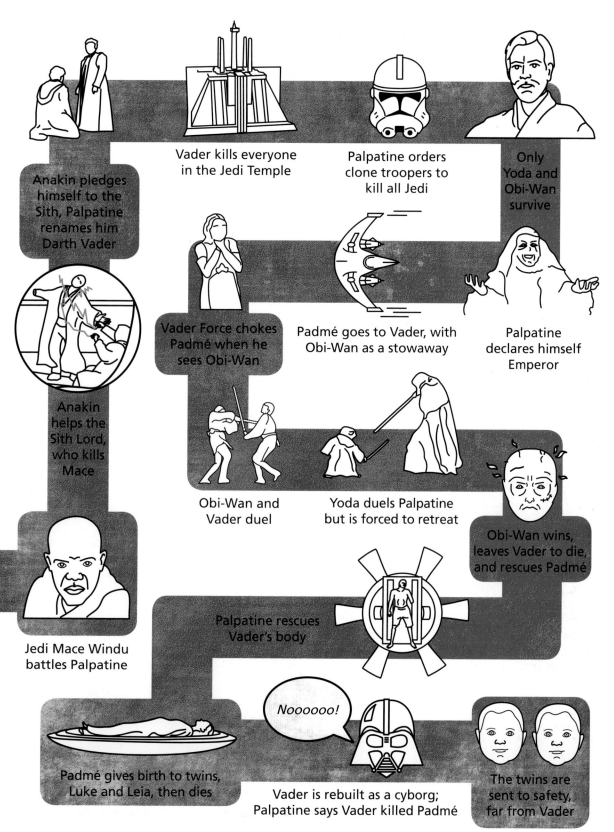

Anakin pledges himself to the Sith, Palpatine renames him Darth Vader

Vader kills everyone in the Jedi Temple

Palpatine orders clone troopers to kill all Jedi

Only Yoda and Obi-Wan survive

Vader Force chokes Padmé when he sees Obi-Wan

Padmé goes to Vader, with Obi-Wan as a stowaway

Palpatine declares himself Emperor

Anakin helps the Sith Lord, who kills Mace

Obi-Wan and Vader duel

Yoda duels Palpatine but is forced to retreat

Obi-Wan wins, leaves Vader to die, and rescues Padmé

Jedi Mace Windu battles Palpatine

Palpatine rescues Vader's body

Noooooo!

Padmé gives birth to twins, Luke and Leia, then dies

Vader is rebuilt as a cyborg; Palpatine says Vader killed Padmé

The twins are sent to safety, far from Vader

EPISODE III: *REVENGE OF THE SITH* A CLOSER LOOK

The third and final film in the prequel trilogy said farewell to Anakin Skywalker and hello to Darth Vader—but not necessarily the Vader we were expecting! This Sith Lord didn't need a mask to strike fear into filmgoers…

THE DARK KNIGHT

Three years into their war with the Galactic Republic, Separatists kidnap the Republic leader, Palpatine. Jedi Knights Anakin Skywalker and Obi-Wan Kenobi rush to save him. With Obi-Wan incapacitated, Anakin fights Count Dooku. Palpatine urges Anakin to kill Dooku; begrudgingly, the Jedi complies.

> ## "Kill him! Kill him now!"
> ### CHANCELLOR PALPATINE

SIDIOUS SURPRISE

Anakin trusts Palpatine and is intrigued by Palpatine's claim that he can teach Anakin how to keep loved ones from dying. Palpatine tells Anakin he is the Sith Lord Darth Sidious, and only he has the power to save Padmé.

Obi-Wan is too busy fighting General Grievous to help the troubled Anakin.

PADMÉ PREMONITION

Having secretly married Anakin three years before, Padmé Amidala is now pregnant. Anakin has nightmares that she will die in childbirth, and vows to save her. To add to his woes, the Jedi ask him to spy on Palpatine, whom they suspect might be the evil Sith Lord that engineered the war.

THE NAME'S VADER

Mace Windu and three other Jedi confront Palpatine (a.k.a. Darth Sidious). Anakin intervenes, fearing that if Sidious is killed, Anakin won't be able to save Padmé. Sidious kills Mace, whereupon Anakin pledges his loyalty to the Sith Lord, who gives him the name Darth Vader.

THE JEDI PURGE: ORDER 66

Sidious sends an order to the Republic's clone troopers, who turn on and kill their Jedi leaders across the galaxy. Vader kills all who remain in the Jedi Temple. Sidious decrees that the Republic is no more. From now on, he will rule the galaxy as his own Empire.

OBI-WAN VS. VADER

Obi-Wan and Yoda are apparently the only Jedi to survive Sidious' purge. Obi-Wan cannot convince Padmé of Anakin's betrayal, so hides on her ship when she goes to him. When Vader sees Obi-Wan in Padmé's ship, he thinks his wife has betrayed him. Vader engages Obi-Wan in a duel, but is defeated and left for dead.

Yoda battles Sidious in the Senate, but the Jedi is eventually forced to flee.

NEW BEGINNINGS

Padmé gives birth to twins before dying. Meanwhile, Sidious retrieves Vader's burned body and rebuilds him as a towering, black-clad cyborg. Sidious tells Vader that Vader killed his pregnant wife in rage. The newborns, Luke and Leia, are sent to new homes to escape Vader's detection.

GOOD GUYS

OBI-WAN KENOBI
Jedi general who believed in Anakin

YODA
Lean, green, survival machine

PADMÉ AMIDALA
A new hope grows within her

MACE WINDU
Dude with the purple lightsaber

BAD GUYS

DARTH VADER
Bad before he wore the helmet

DARTH SIDIOUS
Emperor after all these years

COUNT DOOKU
An apprentice too many for Sidious

GENERAL GRIEVOUS
Wheezing cyborg Separatist

He looks like a pretty kickass robot to me, so…

WHY DOES GENERAL GRIEVOUS COUGH?

OK, I've got some smart tech that can talk, but none of it ever clears its throat to do so. General Grievous is a state-of-the-art bit of kit, so how come he sounds like a wheezy old-timer?

IS HE A ROBOT?

He may be more machine than man, but no: General Grievous is not a robot. He was born to flesh-and-blood parents and is part of a reptilian species called the Kaleesh. Over time, he chose to turn himself into a cyborg.

WHAT'S A CYBORG?

Short for cybernetic organism, a cyborg is a living being that augments its body with technology. If you wear glasses in order to see better, or use a hearing aid to help you hear, you are a very basic cyborg.

SO THE REAL GRIEVOUS IS UNDERNEATH?

What's left of him, yes. He's gone much further than just adding extras to his body: he's had most of it replaced. All that's left underneath the cybernetics is his brain, parts of his head including his eyes, and a few other vital organs, including his heart and lungs.

You must realize you are doomed! <cough>

GENERAL GRIEVOUS

WHY DID HE DO THAT?

Because he wanted to be a better warrior. Back when he had just two arms and an ordinary Kaleesh body, he was a warlord with many enemies. And nothing says "Don't mess" like a cyborg body with four arms, all of them wielding lightsabers.

AREN'T LIGHTSABERS JUST FOR THE SITH AND JEDI?

Usually, yes. But Grievous has a grisly habit of killing Jedi then keeping their weapons for himself. The Jedi-turned-Sith-Lord Count Dooku recruited him to the Separatist cause, then singled him out for lightsaber training.

GEORGE'S MUCUS

The inspiration for Grievous' distinctive sound came from director George Lucas, who had bronchitis during filming!

SO WHY THE COUGHING AND WHEEZING?

Grievous has taken his enhancements to the extreme, and the technology isn't perfect. His respiratory problems are a result of that—as well as being a great way to convey to an audience that he is far from just a robot.

Grievous' piercing yellow eyes are remnants of his original organic form. Like other Kaleesh, he was born a bat-faced, reptilian humanoid.

Grievous can arrange his upper limbs as two or four arms, or use them as legs to scuttle along like a scorpion, with his lower limbs in the air.

Obi-Wan destroys Grievous by firing a blaster through the gaps in his chest armor, igniting the fluid preserving his remaining organs.

PALPATINE IS

We've known it since Episode I, but the rest of the galaxy only finds out in Episode III—Chancellor Palpatine is the Sith Lord Darth Sidious, better known as the Emperor in the original trilogy.

> **"I love democracy. I love the Republic. Once this crisis has abated, I will lay down the powers you have given me!"**
>
> CHANCELLOR PALPATINE TO THE SENATE

- **RULES BY PERSUASION**

- **USES CHARM AS A WEAPON**

- **TRAINS MAUL AND DOOKU**

- **CORRUPTS ANAKIN SKYWALKER**

THE PATH TO POWER

Sheev Palpatine was born with strong Force sensitivity and trained as a Sith Lord from an early age. He was apprenticed to Darth Plagueis, whom he later killed, and kept his powers hidden as he launched his political career. Palpatine rose to be Galactic Senator for his homeworld of Naboo, and manipulated those around him to start a war. He then presented his ascent to Emperor as the only way to stop the war, and was met with thunderous applause.

THE EMPEROR

With his appearance changed as a result of his fight with Mace Windu, Darth Sidious declares himself Emperor of the galaxy. He will rule for 24 years before the rebels bring him down.

> "I have waited a long time for this moment, my little green friend. At last, the Jedi are no more."
>
> *DARTH SIDIOUS TO YODA*

RULES BY DECREE

USES FORCE LIGHTNING

TRAINS DARTH VADER

TRIES TO CORRUPT LUKE

IN THE HOOD

As Emperor, Darth Sidious stays largely out of sight (he's mentioned but not seen in Episode IV), but his influence is everywhere. Vader does his dirty work with an army of stormtroopers that help him lay down the law.

WHY DOES ANAKIN JOIN THE DARK SIDE?

We've followed him from childhood through his troubled teens, and now he's a Jedi Knight. I know he's done some bad stuff, but I'm still rooting for him. So why does he have to turn so bad?

DOES HE DO IT FOR LOVE?

He would say so, yes. But while his love for Padmé is a deeply held passion, it is rarely concerned with her best interests. Raised as a slave with nothing to call his own, then deprived of his mother, Anakin mostly sees Padmé in terms of his own needs. He guards her jealously, and rages against the idea of death taking her away from him. He is afraid of life without her.

SO IT'S OUT OF FEAR?

Also yes. As a child, he had no control over events, and while the Jedi strive to teach him self-control, he remains fearful of the disorder around him. While Darth Sidious revels in chaos, Anakin craves order, and becomes willing to impose it by any means necessary.

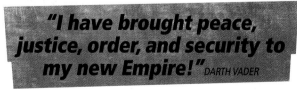

"I have brought peace, justice, order, and security to my new Empire!" DARTH VADER

ANAKIN SKYWALKER

IS IT A MISTAKE?

Definitely yes! But if you mean, "Is he tricked into joining the dark side?" then no. Sidious manipulates him so he has to make a choice, but the choice is all Anakin's own. He is no stranger to the dark side, either, having killed in anger on more than one occasion.

IS IT FATE?

In that his choice could never have been different? Perhaps. The Force moves in mysterious ways, and he was seen as the Chosen One who would bring balance to the Force. His actions lead to the Jedi numbering no more than the Sith, so the prophesy comes true, in a way.

IS HE JUST BAD?

No, and that's the tragedy of Darth Vader. We all give in to anger, fear, and passion sometimes, but it doesn't make us bad people. Anakin was a great Jedi. He just happened to make a great Sith Lord, too.

EVOLUTION OF ANAKIN

Slave

Padawan

Jedi Knight

Still a Padawan

Darth Vader

Vader redeemed

When Vader Force-chokes Padmé, any hope for Anakin is gone. The anger Sidious urged him to embrace has been given free rein to consume him.

Remade and remodeled by Darth Sidious' droids, Vader spends his later life encased in armor, both a life-support system and a statement of intent.

I know they're just obeying orders, but…

WHY DO THE CLONES KILL ALL THE JEDI?

The clone troopers are fighting alongside the Jedi, and then suddenly they're fighting against the Jedi! How can they just switch sides?

WHO CONTROLS THE CLONE TROOPERS?

Ultimately, Chancellor Palpatine controls the clone army, having secretly funded their development and specified the finer points of their design. It's true that they have been bred to obey the Jedi, but only for as long as Palpatine allows it.

DON'T THE CLONES HAVE FREE WILL?

They do, and that's what makes them superior to battle droids. But their brains have been altered to make them more obedient than the original human from which they are all descended. What the Jedi don't realize is that a chip has been implanted in each trooper's brain requiring all clones to obey Order 66.

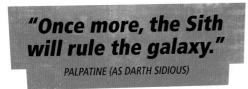

"Once more, the Sith will rule the galaxy."

PALPATINE (AS DARTH SIDIOUS)

WHAT IS ORDER 66?

Order 66 is the instruction to kill all Jedi. As soon as a clone trooper receives the order, it flips a switch in his brain, making him turn on his former commanders.

WHY DOES IT WORK?

Given that we've seen Jedi get out of worse scrapes, you mean? Because this time, the Jedi are focused on fighting the Separatist droid army. They have no reason to suspect their obedient troops, who have served them well for three years. Every Jedi leads many troopers so when they turn, the Jedi are totally surrounded and outnumbered.

HOW DOES PALPATINE GET AWAY WITH IT?

He's a popular and lawfully elected leader, while the Jedi are a secretive sect. When Palpatine says the Jedi tried to kill him and he has the scars to prove it, no one has any reason to doubt the Jedi's treachery.

HOW TO BECOME EMPEROR: THE PALPATINE WAY

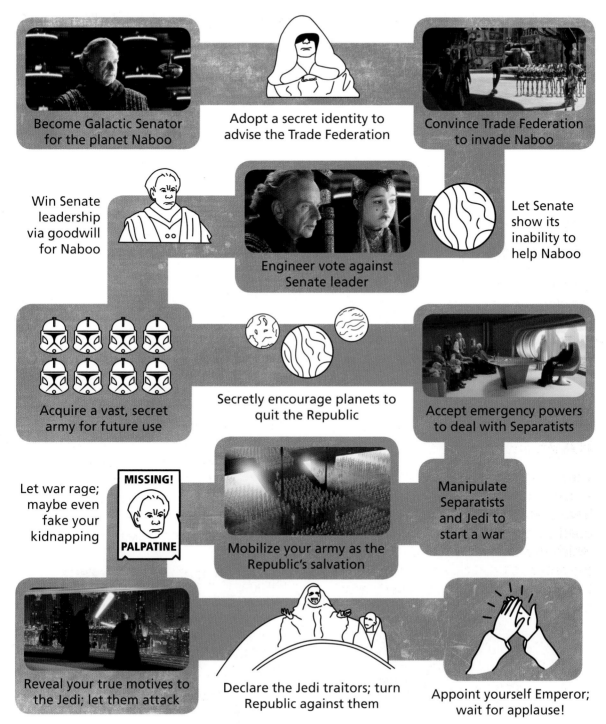

Become Galactic Senator for the planet Naboo

Adopt a secret identity to advise the Trade Federation

Convince Trade Federation to invade Naboo

Win Senate leadership via goodwill for Naboo

Engineer vote against Senate leader

Let Senate show its inability to help Naboo

Acquire a vast, secret army for future use

Secretly encourage planets to quit the Republic

Accept emergency powers to deal with Separatists

Let war rage; maybe even fake your kidnapping

MISSING!

PALPATINE

Mobilize your army as the Republic's salvation

Manipulate Separatists and Jedi to start a war

Reveal your true motives to the Jedi; let them attack

Declare the Jedi traitors; turn Republic against them

Appoint yourself Emperor; wait for applause!

BATTLE OF CORUSCANT
MADE SIMPLE

Sometimes you gotta go all-in or go home. That was the mind-set behind Count Dooku and General Grievous' attack on the Republic's capital. It doesn't quite work out.

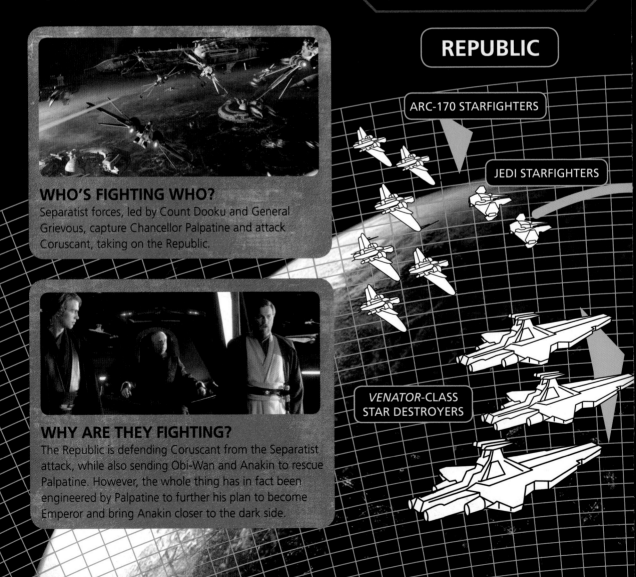

WHO'S FIGHTING WHO?

Separatist forces, led by Count Dooku and General Grievous, capture Chancellor Palpatine and attack Coruscant, taking on the Republic.

WHY ARE THEY FIGHTING?

The Republic is defending Coruscant from the Separatist attack, while also sending Obi-Wan and Anakin to rescue Palpatine. However, the whole thing has in fact been engineered by Palpatine to further his plan to become Emperor and bring Anakin closer to the dark side.

REPUBLIC

ARC-170 STARFIGHTERS

JEDI STARFIGHTERS

VENATOR-CLASS STAR DESTROYERS

KEY MOMENT

DEADLY DUEL—Anakin engages in a duel with Count Dooku, tapping into the dark side to overpower him and cut off his hands. With encouragement from Palpatine, Anakin kills Dooku in cold blood—an act against the Jedi code.

WHO WINS?

On the surface, the Republic. Palpatine is rescued, Count Dooku is killed, and General Grievous flees with the few remaining Separatist ships.

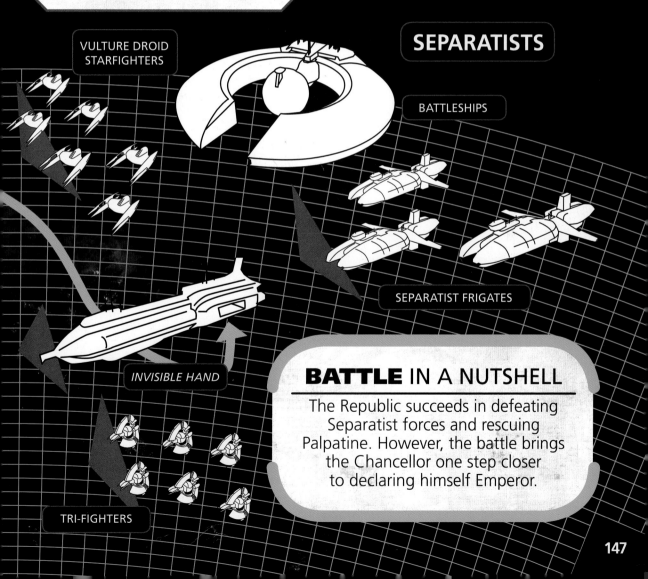

VULTURE DROID STARFIGHTERS

SEPARATISTS

BATTLESHIPS

SEPARATIST FRIGATES

INVISIBLE HAND

BATTLE IN A NUTSHELL

The Republic succeeds in defeating Separatist forces and rescuing Palpatine. However, the battle brings the Chancellor one step closer to declaring himself Emperor.

TRI-FIGHTERS

147

STAR WARS *ON TV:*
STAR WARS: THE CLONE WARS *AND* STAR WARS REBELS

> ## *"Changed, something has."*
>
> YODA

The movies are the heart of the saga, but the animated TV shows provide a lot of soul. *Star Wars: The Clone Wars* reveals the epic battles that occur between **Episodes II and III**, and *Star Wars Rebels* sets the stage for *Rogue One* and Episode IV.

Want to know more about Anakin's adventures? Then check out…

STAR WARS: THE CLONE WARS

Set between Episodes II and III, animated TV series Star Wars: The Clone Wars *showed Anakin Skywalker's glory days as a Jedi Knight—a story that fans always wanted to see.*

ANAKIN'S APPRENTICE

With no *Star Wars* movies made since 2005, *Star Wars: The Clone Wars* was a digitally animated dream come true when it debuted in 2008. The series ran for six seasons to 2014, with 121 half-hour episodes linking into story arcs that shed light on many aspects of the *Star Wars* universe. Central to the series is the relationship between Jedi Knight Anakin Skywalker and his Padawan sidekick—a kickass new character named Ahsoka Tano.

Ahsoka has distinctive facial markings and long, striped head tails. She is notable as the first female Force user to have a starring role in the *Star Wars* story.

Making individual clones into identifiable heroes adds resonance to their betrayal of the Jedi in Episode III. Bred to obey, their allegiance can be changed in an instant.

SEND IN THE CLONES

The series features many familiar characters, such as Obi-Wan, Yoda, and Grievous, but also gives screen time to the ground troops that give the show its name. Clones such as Cody, who appear briefly in Episode III, are given complex, compelling story arcs—as well as plenty of front-line action!

"We're not programmed."
CAPTAIN REX

MAUL STANDS TALL

As well as old friends, *The Clone Wars* revisits old enemies, including Darth Maul. He may have been chopped in half in Episode I, but now his top half is back—with mighty robot legs! The show also introduces new bad guys, such as bounty hunter Cad Bane and badass woman warrior Asajj Ventress.

Maul's hatred for the Jedi kept him alive, even though he'd been sliced in two! After years of madness and suffering, he sets out to wreak revenge on Obi-Wan Kenobi.

MORE TO SAY

With more room to explore *Star Wars* mythology than any single movie, the show sheds new light on much more than just the Clone Wars themselves. We meet Force users who are neither Jedi nor Sith, and learn more about the Force itself when Yoda embarks on a mystical quest. We see more of life within the Jedi Order, and how it is ill-equipped to deal with the Sith threat, and we get a better sense of Anakin's slow descent into darkness. Treat yourself to a binge-watch and see *Star Wars* in a whole new way!

GOOD GUYS

ANAKIN SKYWALKER
Jedi who doesn't
want a Padawan

AHSOKA TANO
Padawan out to
prove herself

CAPTAIN REX
A face you'll be
seeing a lot of

OBI-WAN KENOBI
He fought in
the Clone Wars

BAD GUYS

**CHANCELLOR
PALPATINE**
Secret Sith Lord

ASAJJ VENTRESS
Dark side assassin and
spooky Nightsister

CAD BANE
Bad man with
a good hat

SAVAGE OPRESS
Think Darth Maul's
bad? Meet his brother!

A small band of heroes holds out against the Empire in...

STAR WARS REBELS

The prequel movies predated the Rebellion, while the original trilogy showed the Rebel Alliance at its peak. Now, animated adventure Star Wars Rebels slots neatly between the two, showing the rise of the rebels in smaller installments.

CELL MATES

Launched in 2014, digitally animated TV series *Star Wars Rebels* follows a rag-tag band of freedom fighters out to give the Empire a bloody nose. Set five years before the events of Episode IV: *A New Hope*, there is not yet a Rebel Alliance to rely on—but there is a growing network of rebel cells, of which our heroes are a part. Of course, the Empire is out to crush the Rebellion before it begins, and it's not long before the rebels attract some pretty high-profile attention.

The *Ghost* gets its name from an array of stealth tech that makes it almost invisible to sensors. Its on-board shuttle goes by the similarly spooky name of *Phantom*.

GHOST RIDERS

The core team of rebels are Kanan, Ezra, Hera, Sabine, Zeb, and Chopper, who travel on a ship called the *Ghost*. Kanan was a Jedi Padawan who is now training Ezra to use the Force. Revealing his Jedi skills leads the Empire to send its fearsome, Force-wielding Inquisitors after the *Ghost* crew. In time, this little ship proves such a thorn in the Empire's side that the crew also clash with Darth Vader and an Imperial Grand Admiral by the name of Thrawn.

The rebels all have beef with the Empire, having seen its worst excesses up close. Hera, Chopper, and Kanan were the first to team up, with Ezra the most recent recruit.

Grand Admiral Thrawn surrounds himself with cultural artifacts that give him insight as to how his enemies will behave, then calmly watches his predictions play out.

BOOK BADDIE

There are many familiar faces in *Star Wars Rebels*, with Princess Leia, Lando Calrissian, Darth Maul, clone trooper Captain Rex, Saw Gerrera, and Ahsoka Tano from *Star Wars: The Clone Wars* all putting in appearances. Introduced in Season Three, the big bad guy is intellectual Imperial Thrawn—a long-time fan favorite introduced in a series of *Star Wars* novels in the 1990s.

MORE LORE

Like *Star Wars: The Clone Wars* before it, *Rebels* takes full advantage of its ongoing TV format to go deeper into *Star Wars* lore. It shows the realities of life under the Empire, and explores strange new ways of using the Force. It also reveals when Anakin's former Jedi Padawan Ahsoka Tano learns the truth about Darth Vader!

> **"Do you know what I've become?"** *DARTH VADER*

GOOD GUYS

KANAN JARRUS
Jedi who survived Palpatine's purge

EZRA BRIDGER
Street thief turned Kanan's Padawan

HERA SYNDULLA
Peerless pilot and captain of the *Ghost*

SABINE WREN
Graffiti artist and explosives expert

ZEB ORRELIOS
Kind of like a less hairy Wookiee

CHOPPER
Badly behaved droid, a.k.a. C1-10P

BAD GUYS

GRAND INQUISITOR
Former Jedi turned Jedi hunter

GRAND ADMIRAL THRAWN
Bright blue brainiac

EPISODE VII:
THE FORCE AWAKENS

"Chewie, we're home."

HAN TO CHEWIE

EPISODE VII: *THE FORCE AWAKENS* AT A GLANCE

The planet Jakku

Poe Dameron receives map that leads to missing Luke

Meet the new bad guy in town— Kylo Ren

Kylo Ren's stormtroopers capture Poe

Finn and Poe separated in crash on Jakku

Stormtrooper Finn helps Poe escape

BB-8 teams up with scavenger Rey

Poe's droid, BB-8, escapes with map

Fugitive Finn befriends Rey and BB-8

Han is Kylo Ren's dad!

Han and co. visit Maz Kanata on Takodana

Ren captures Rey and takes her to Starkiller Base

They flee Jakku in a beat-up old ship

The ship's owners, Han and Chewie, turn up

Rey finds Luke's lightsaber in Maz's castle and has a vision

Starkiller Base destroys Republic capital

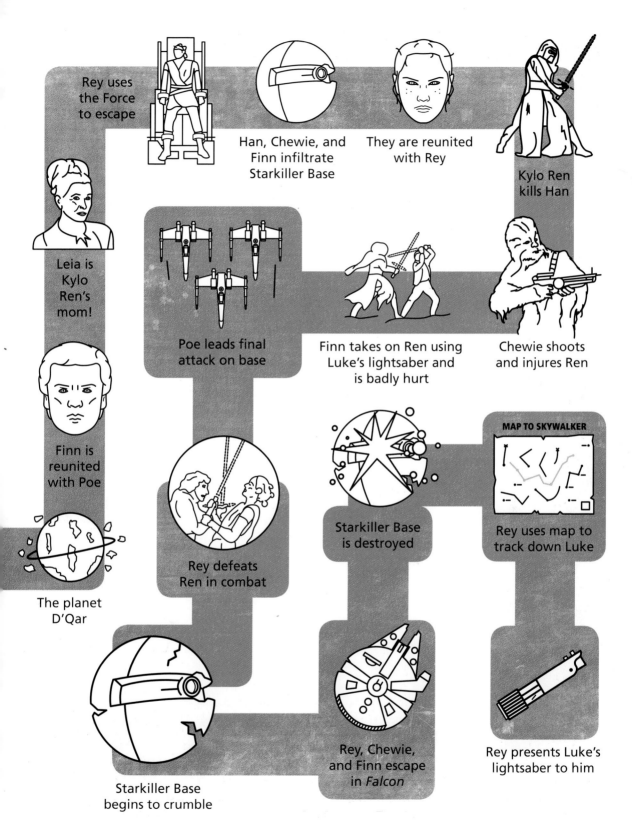

Rey uses the Force to escape

Han, Chewie, and Finn infiltrate Starkiller Base

They are reunited with Rey

Kylo Ren kills Han

Leia is Kylo Ren's mom!

Poe leads final attack on base

Finn takes on Ren using Luke's lightsaber and is badly hurt

Chewie shoots and injures Ren

Finn is reunited with Poe

MAP TO SKYWALKER

Rey defeats Ren in combat

Starkiller Base is destroyed

Rey uses map to track down Luke

The planet D'Qar

Starkiller Base begins to crumble

Rey, Chewie, and Finn escape in *Falcon*

Rey presents Luke's lightsaber to him

157

EPISODE VII: *THE FORCE AWAKENS* A CLOSER LOOK

When the Empire came to an end, the galaxy deserved a break. But after a well-earned rest, Han, Chewie, and Leia were back in action again. They teamed up with a new generation of heroes and took the fight to the fearsome First Order…

A NEW ORDER

Luke Skywalker has disappeared. His sister, Leia, is desperate to find him as she leads the Resistance against the evil First Order, which has risen from the ashes of the Empire.

LOOKING FOR LUKE

On the planet Jakku, Resistance pilot Poe Dameron acquires part of a map showing Luke's location. He is captured by First Order stormtroopers, but his droid, BB-8, gets away with the map and teams up with a hardy young scavenger called Rey.

Masked Force user Kylo Ren leads the stormtroopers that capture Poe.

FINN AND THE *FALCON*

Poe escapes with help from a reluctant stormtrooper, FN-2187, whom he dubs Finn. They steal a ship, only to crash in another part of Jakku. With no sign of Poe, Finn goes it alone and runs into Rey and BB-8. The First Order attacks, and the trio flee Jakku in a beat-up old ship: the *Millennium Falcon*.

SOLO SAYS

Detecting the *Falcon* in flight, Han Solo and Chewie reclaim their old ship. They study BB-8's map to Luke, but find it is incomplete. Han says that Luke disappeared after his new Jedi Order was wiped out by one of his pupils who fell to the dark side. That dark side Force user was Kylo Ren, who just happens to be Han Solo's son!

TROUBLE ON TAKODANA

Han and co. go to Takodana to find the Resistance. Meanwhile, Rey finds Luke's lightsaber, but refuses to take it, even when Han's old friend Maz Kanata tells her to. The First Order attacks, but the Resistance saves Han and Chewie, who are reunited with Leia, and Finn, who is reunited with Poe. Rey is not so lucky, and is taken prisoner by Ren.

The First Order strikes from a weaponized planetoid known as Starkiller Base.

A DEATH IN THE FAMILY

Rey escapes into Starkiller Base in time to meet Han, Chewie, and Finn as they set up explosives to bring down the shield. Han encounters his son, Kylo Ren, and implores him to renounce the dark side, but instead Ren kills him. Chewie shoots Ren, injuring him, then sets off the explosives. Finn tries to fight Ren but is badly wounded. Rey uses the Force to defeat him, and the base disintegrates as Resistance fighters attack. Chewie and Rey escape with a comatose Finn.

NEW HOPES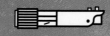

As Rey, Chewie, and Leia mourn Han, the long-dormant droid R2-D2 "wakes up" and reveals the rest of BB-8's map. Rey finds Luke alone on a distant world, and presents him with his lightsaber.

GOOD GUYS

REY
Scavenger, waiting for family

FINN
Stormtrooper, swaps sides

POE DAMERON
Finn's first Resistance pal

LEIA ORGANA
Resistance leader and baddie's mom

HAN SOLO
Smuggler and baddie's dad

LUKE SKYWALKER
Brave Jedi, almost not in this film

BAD GUYS

KYLO REN
A villain of the First Order

SNOKE
Ren's shadowy Supreme Leader

It acts like the Empire, but it's not the Empire, so…

WHAT ACTUALLY IS THE FIRST ORDER?

Last thing I heard, Ewoks were dancing on the Empire's grave. How come stormtroopers and planet-sized superweapons are back in fashion in The Force Awakens?

WHERE DID THE FIRST ORDER COME FROM?

After the death of the Emperor and the destruction of the second Death Star, the Empire was, like, *so* over. A New Republic took its place and 30 years of galactic peace ensued. But for some people, the Empire never went out of fashion. Former Imperial leaders and their sympathizers regrouped in secret and set themselves up with a new army. Now they refer to themselves as "the First Order" and serve a powerful new leader known only as Snoke.

WHO IS SNOKE?

No one knows much about the Supreme Leader of the First Order, except that he is not likely to win any beauty contests. He is a twisted, gray figure who gives his orders remotely, and relies on Kylo Ren to enact his will. He lured Ren to the dark side and continues to train him, as well as overseeing the First Order military.

WHAT DOES THE FIRST ORDER WANT?

Power, of course! It wants to rule through force and fear, and basically recreate the bad old days of the Empire. That means using its army of stormtroopers to overthrow the New Republic. It also means destroying Luke Skywalker and his hopes for a new Jedi Order, as the Jedi would defend the Republic against attack and make the First Order's job even harder.

The First Order military is made up of a new generation of stormtroopers, brainwashed from childhood to serve and obey without question.

IS THE NEW REPUBLIC FIGHTING BACK?

Not really. Ever since the Empire fell, the New Republic has promoted peace through disarmament. Now its Senate is split between those unwilling to risk that peace, others who don't think the First Order poses a serious threat, and some who actually admire the former Empire and would like to see it return! Senator Leia Organa grew so frustrated by this stalemate that she formed her own resistance movement. Its mission is to make sure the First Order obeys galactic law, and to prove to the Galactic Senate when it doesn't.

> **"The First Order rose from the dark side."**
>
> LOR SAN TEKKA

IS IT WORKING?

The Resistance might have succeeded in making the Senate see that the First Order was up to no good… if the First Order hadn't blown up the entire Senate along with the New Republic capital, Hosnian Prime, using their secret Starkiller Base. That made any argument fairly pointless, and initiated open warfare.

The First Order used Starkiller Base to destroy Hosnian Prime, firing stellar energy through hyperspace to incinerate the planet from afar.

WHAT IS STARKILLER BASE?

The First Order's fearsome flagship is a whole planet repurposed as a weapon. It makes the Death Star seem positively quaint!

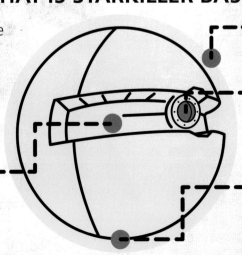

MAGNETIC CORE
A vast array of energy collectors sucks the power out of a sun and stores it in the planet's core.

ENERGY SHIELD
Protects the entire planet from attack.

SUPERWEAPON
Channels the stellar energy from the core at an unsuspecting target via hyperspace.

THERMAL OSCILLATOR
Generates a containment field to help contain the stellar energy within.

The new man in black is definitely not Darth Vader...

WHO IS KYLO REN?

Darth Vader is dead and the Empire is no more. So who's this moody, masked figure strutting around like Return of the Jedi *never happened?*

IS KYLO REN A SITH LORD?

No, but he might just be their biggest fan. He dresses in black, wields a red lightsaber, and uses the dark side of the Force in emulation of his hero and grandfather, Darth Vader.

SO WHY THE VADER VIBES?

Ren has been led astray by a mysterious being called Snoke, the Supreme Leader of the First Order. Snoke wants to revive the age of Empire, and saw Ren's potential as his apprentice, given that he is Darth Vader's grandson.

GRANDSON?

Kylo Ren is the son of Han Solo and Leia, born shortly after the Empire fell. As you'll recall, Leia turned out to be Luke's twin sister, making Darth Vader her father. She and Han called their son Ben, and he inherited the family's connection to the Force.

KYLO REN

162

WHY DOES HE CALL HIMSELF KYLO REN?

On turning to the dark side, Ben joined the Knights of Ren—a menacing band of warriors. Like his Sith Lord idol, he took a new name that reflected his change in allegiance and made a break with his past.

SO HE DOESN'T GET ON WITH MOM AND DAD?

Ren is more than just estranged from his parents, he actually kills Han Solo at the end of the film!

YIKES! WHO TRAINED HIM TO USE THE FORCE?

That was his Uncle Luke. He was trying to start a new Jedi Order, and Ben was an obvious candidate—having untapped power and a clear need for discipline in his troubled youth. However, Ben turned on his fellow trainees, killing them all. He joined the First Order with his training far from complete, and Luke went into self-imposed exile.

WILL HE COME GOOD IN THE END, THOUGH?

Well, he hasn't done so far. It's a hard road back to the light side when you've killed your dad and one of the *Star Wars* saga's biggest heroes. But if he really idolizes his gramps, let's hope he knows that even Vader renounced the dark side in the end—and Vader let the Death Star destroy an entire planet!

Kylo Ren's lightsaber is powered by a cracked and unstable kyber crystal. Its crossguard design helps balance its power—as well as looking cool!

Beneath his mask, Ren is fully human. He wears it as armor, and to emulate his grandfather, Darth Vader.

I'm feeling a bit far out of my depth again, so...

WHO IS REY?

Is she the new hope that will bring about the return of the Jedi, or is she just lucky when it comes to handling a lightsaber?

> The Jedi were real?

WHY DOES REY LIVE IN AN AT-AT?

Rey was abandoned in the wastes of Jakku when she was very young. She grew up alone and scavenged to survive, learning to make good use of the Graveyard of Giants, a vast plain of crashed starships left behind after the last battle between the Rebel Alliance and the Empire. A downed AT-AT is borderline luxury when you're forced to live in those conditions.

WHY DOES SHE STAY IN THE DESERT?

She's in no position to go anywhere else. Apart from having no friends on Jakku, she is very poor, living off the meager food rations she can get from trader Unkar Plutt in exchange for salvage. Sure, she eventually gets away by stealing an old ship, but that gets her into a whole new heap of trouble—as she no doubt knew it would.

REY

HOW DOES REY KNOW HOW TO FLY THE *FALCON*?

You'd be amazed what you can learn when you have a desert full of Imperial tech to play with. Also, the *Millennium Falcon* may have been grounded, but luckily many of the computer functions on it still work—including flight controls and simulators.

WHY DOES SHE HAVE A VISION WHEN SHE FINDS LUKE'S LIGHTSABER?

Rey has a strong sensitivity to the Force, but has never encountered its power in the deserts of Jakku. There could hardly be a more Force-filled object than Luke's first lightsaber (which also belonged to Anakin Skywalker), so Rey's exposure to it is overwhelming. The wise Maz Kanata says the blade is calling to Rey, and it obviously has a lot to say!

HOW IS SHE ABLE TO USE THE FORCE?

Young Anakin Skywalker and Princess Leia both showed a basic ability to use the Force without training—though not as a conscious decision. Rey's ability to employ Jedi mind tricks and wield a lightsaber shows off her prodigious natural talent, proving that she can instinctively use the Force, even without training. Who knows what she will be able to do next…

Trader Unkar Plutt takes advantage of Rey's talent for finding valuable salvage, but as he is her only source of rations, she is unable to object.

Rey's Force sensitivity draws her to Luke's lightsaber, which shows her visions of Luke, her own past, and an encounter with Kylo Ren in her future.

When she faces Kylo Ren on the disintegrating surface of Starkiller Base, Rey draws on the Force to best him in her very first lightsaber duel.

Rey and Ren aren't the only newbies in The Force Awakens

ALSO INTRODUCING IN EPISODE VII...

The Force Awakens *is packed full of new characters. Some team up with familiar old friends, while others pose fresh dangers. Here are four you need to know…*

MAGIC 8-BALL

Director J.J. Abrams named BB-8 based on the droid's figure-eight shape!

FINN

The First Order took Finn from his family when he was very young and raised him to be a stormtrooper. But he flees when he is ordered to kill, and teams up with Rey and BB-8 instead. At first, he isn't sure about joining the Resistance, but he ends up dueling with Kylo Ren!

POE DAMERON

Brave Resistance pilot Poe goes to Jakku to fetch a map that leads to Luke Skywalker. He gets captured by the First Order, but manages to send the map to safety first. Finn helps him escape from the First Order, and Poe returns the favor later on, when Kylo Ren attacks Finn and co. on Takodana.

BB-8

Entrusted with a vital clue to Luke Skywalker's location, Poe Dameron's droid treks across Jakku before rolling into a new friend, Rey. He draws Rey and Finn into a race across the galaxy to reach the Resistance, before being reunited with Poe to attack Starkiller Base.

CAPTAIN PHASMA

Phasma is Finn's captain when the First Order attacks Jakku. She orders all the civilians killed, then calls for Finn to be mentally reconditioned when he doesn't comply with orders. Finn gets his revenge later on, when he takes her prisoner on Starkiller Base and forces her to drop the station's shields.

ASSAULT ON STARKILLER BASE
MADE SIMPLE

Oh tyrants of the galaxy. When will you learn that bigger is not necessarily better? Starkiller Base dwarfs the old Death Stars, but it has the same vulnerabilities...

RESISTANCE

X-WINGS

MILLENNIUM FALCON

WHO'S FIGHTING WHO?
The Resistance has launched its X-wings, led by Poe Dameron, in an effort to destroy the First Order's Starkiller Base once and for all.

INFO BOX

LOCATION—A mobile ice planet, Starkiller Base, housing a superweapon

TERRAIN—Snowy forest on the surface

FORCES—Resistance fleet and First Order army

WHY ARE THEY FIGHTING?
The First Order used Starkiller Base to destroy the Hosnian system, which was the capital of the New Republic. The mobile planet is now closing in on the Resistance base at D'Qar. The Resistance must act first before it is wiped out completely.

FIRST ORDER

TIE FIGHTERS

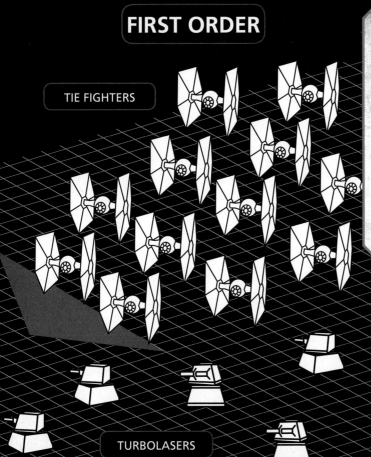

KEY MOMENT

COLLAPSE—Poe Dameron flies toward the thermal oscillator at the center of Starkiller Base, firing torpedoes to destroy it, and thus the entire base.

TURBOLASERS

BATTLE IN A NUTSHELL

Destroying Starkiller Base is a great victory for the Resistance. However, after the destruction of the New Republic, the Resistance still has a lot of work to do to protect the galaxy from the oppressive First Order.

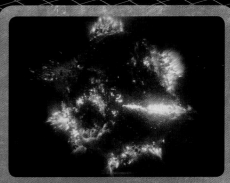

WHO WINS?

With the oscillator destroyed, Starkiller Base explodes. It's a massive victory for the Resistance, but General Hux, Phasma, and Kylo Ren all escape to fight another day.

"Rebellions are built on hope." *JYN ERSO*

ROGUE ONE: A STAR WARS STORY AT A GLANCE

Krennic kills Jyn's mom, kidnaps dad

Saw Gerrera takes in young Jyn

Years pass, Jyn is in prison

Cassian goes to kill him, but relents

Now free, Jyn goes on a mission with a group of rebels

Imperial defector Bodhi brings message to Saw

Cassian learns that Empire is building a "planet killer"

Jyn, Bodhi, and co. locate Jyn's dad on Eadu

The planet Jedha

They are helped by Chirrut and Baze

Message from Jyn's dad

Jyn and Cassian seek out Saw

He hid a fatal flaw in the Death Star

Death Star destroys the Holy City and Saw

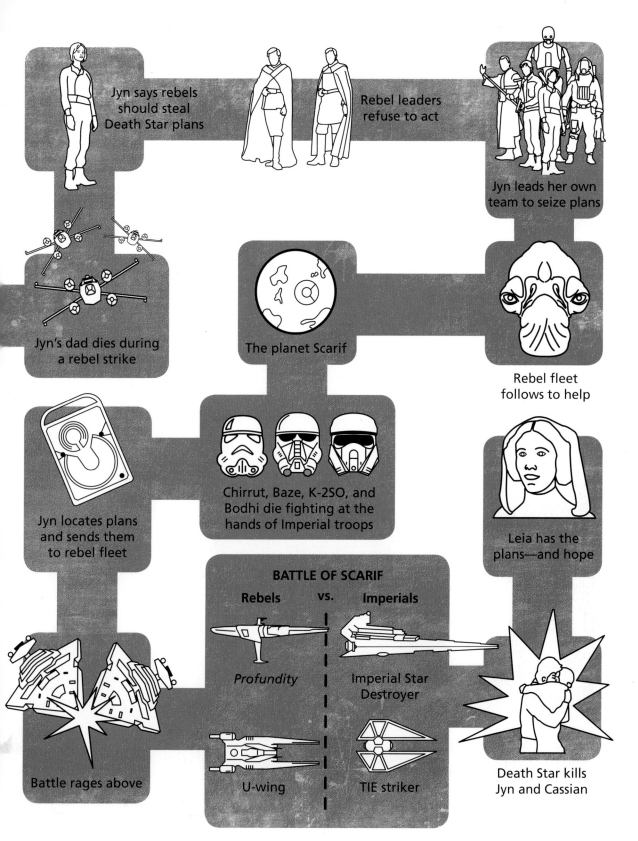

Jyn says rebels should steal Death Star plans

Rebel leaders refuse to act

Jyn leads her own team to seize plans

Jyn's dad dies during a rebel strike

The planet Scarif

Rebel fleet follows to help

Jyn locates plans and sends them to rebel fleet

Chirrut, Baze, K-2SO, and Bodhi die fighting at the hands of Imperial troops

Leia has the plans—and hope

BATTLE OF SCARIF

Rebels vs. **Imperials**

Profundity

Imperial Star Destroyer

U-wing

TIE striker

Battle rages above

Death Star kills Jyn and Cassian

ROGUE ONE: A STAR WARS STORY A CLOSER LOOK

The first Star Wars *movie with no Skywalkers among its major characters,* Rogue One: A Star Wars Story *stood alone as a different kind of adventure—one where heroes were harder to come by, and didn't always want the job.*

A CHILD OF THE EMPIRE

Young Jyn Erso escapes when Imperial big shot Orson Krennic comes for her family. Her mom is killed and her dad is pressed into service as a scientist for the Empire. Jyn is taken in and raised by the rebel extremist Saw Gerrera.

REBEL RECRUIT

Thirteen years later, cargo pilot Bodhi Rook defects from the Empire and brings a recorded message from Jyn's dad, Galen, to Saw Gerrera. Knowing that Jyn was once close to Saw, the Rebel Alliance breaks her out of jail and sends her to see him— as a route to finding Galen and (unknown to Jyn) killing him.

> **"Your behavior, Jyn Erso, is continually unexpected."** *K-2SO*

FATHER FIGURES

On the planet Jedha, warriors Chirrut Îmwe and Baze Malbus help Jyn and her rebel minder Cassian Andor as they seek out Saw. When they find him, he shows Jyn her dad's message. Galen says he has built a flaw into the Empire's new super-weapon—the Death Star—and the plans are at an Imperial base on the planet Scarif.

The Death Star targets Jedha City, and Jyn, Cassian, Bodhi, Chirrut, Baze, and rebel droid K-2SO flee together. Saw stays behind to die.

LOST AND FOUND

Cassian, Jyn, and co. locate Galen on the planet Eadu at an Imperial research base. Cassian sets out to kill him, but relents. However, Galen is mortally wounded in a surprise rebel attack. He and Jyn are briefly reunited before he dies.

ROGUE RAIDERS

Jyn challenges the rebel leaders to act on her dad's information, but they dare not. Instead, she leads a crew of rogues and rebels in a raid on Scarif. When some in the Alliance realize this, part of the fleet races to Scarif to support them.

Jyn's crew travels to Scarif in a stolen Imperial ship. Asked for a call sign prior to departure to Scarif, Bodhi replies "Rogue One."

HOPE HAS A PRICE

Jyn and Cassian acquire the Death Star plans, but at the cost of many lives, including Chirrut, Baze, Bodhi, and K-2SO. They face off with Krennic before Jyn manages to send the plans to the other rebels in orbit. The Death Star targets Scarif, killing Jyn, Cassian, and Krennic, but they are too late. The rebels have the plans, and hope for the future.

GOOD GUYS

JYN ERSO
Rebel in need
of a cause

CASSIAN ANDOR
Rebel, soldier,
spy, assassin

K-2SO
Droid with an
attitude problem

BODHI ROOK
Imperial pilot
turned rebel

CHIRRUT ÎMWE
Warrior monk and
Force follower

BAZE MALBUS
Loyal friend who
lost his faith

BAD GUYS

ORSON KRENNIC
Director of Death
Star weaponry

WILHUFF TARKIN
Top man on
the Death Star

Rogue One *was released after Episode VII, so...*

WHY ISN'T THIS EPISODE VIII?

OK. I've got the sequence now. It goes four-five-six, one-two-three, seven-eight. How did I never guess? But even though there is a number eight, Rogue One *isn't it. Right?*

WHAT MAKES A *STAR WARS* FILM AN EPISODE?

To recap, the episodes of the *Star Wars* saga are the movies that tell the story of the Skywalkers. Episodes I–III follow the life of Anakin Skywalker from early childhood to his "death" in the shadow of Darth Vader. Episodes IV–VI have Luke Skywalker and his journey from farmboy to Jedi at their heart, as well as the redemption of Darth Vader. Episode VII onward explores the Skywalker legacy, which includes the search for Luke and the addition of his nephew, and Leia's son, Kylo Ren.

SO WHAT IS *ROGUE ONE*?

Rogue One is, to give it its full title, *A Star Wars Story*. It's the first in a series of films that will delve into the wider *Star Wars* world in ways that may touch on the Skywalker saga, but do not directly develop it. So even though the plot of *Rogue One* ties in closely with events in Episode IV, neither film relies on the other to be understood and enjoyed.

JYN ERSO

> **"Now they're going to Scarif? Why does no one tell me anything?"** *C-3PO*

Instead of the familiar music and "opening crawl" of text floating in space, *Rogue One* treads its own path right from the outset.

SO... WHAT'S THE POINT?

Even though you don't need to see *Rogue One* to fully understand what's going on in the episodes, doing so will add an extra level of satisfaction when you spot ways in which the two strands overlap. *Rogue One* and future standalone movies also provide an opportunity to go places and explore themes in the *Star Wars* universe that the already epic episode structure simply can't fit in.

Episode IV sowed the seeds for *Rogue One* in 1977, with the Death Star plans already stolen by unknown rebels at the start of the film.

WHAT'S NEXT IN THE STANDALONE SERIES?

The next movie will be about the adventures of young Han Solo and Lando Calrissian, as well as Chewbacca, the *Millennium Falcon*, and a slew of cool new characters.

EXCITING! WHEN WILL I GET TO SEE THAT?

Standalone movies are set to be released every other year, in between the episodes. With Episode VIII: *The Last Jedi* landing in 2017, followed by Episode IX in 2019, you can expect to make a date with young Han in 2018.

Look closely, and you'll spot unused footage from Episode IV intercut with new material during *Rogue One*'s climactic Battle of Scarif.

THE REBELS OF ROGUE ONE

Set just before Episode IV: A New Hope, *there are a lot of new faces in* Rogue One: A Star Wars Story. *They belong to a group of rebels who help further the fight to take down the Empire—but who are they?*

JYN ERSO

Her dad called her "Stardust," but there's nothing twinkly about this rebel-turned-crook-turned-rebel-again. Jyn has little time for the rebel cause, even when the Alliance frees her from prison. But when she sees a message from her father, who has helped design an Imperial superweapon, everything changes.

CHIRRUT ÎMWE

One of the warrior monks known as the Guardians of the Whills, Chirrut is blind and relies on his unshakeable belief in the Force to guide him in all things.

CASSIAN ANDOR

A rebel spy and soldier, Captain Cassian Andor is a man willing to do whatever it takes to defeat the Empire—even if it means killing his own informants.

BAZE MALBUS

Once a warrior monk like Chirrut, Baze lost his faith, and devoted himself to fighting the Empire. He stood by his friend Chirrut, however, and the pair make a formidable team.

BODHI ROOK

A cargo pilot who sympathized with the rebels, Bodhi carried a vital message from Jyn's father to Saw Gerrera, only to be tortured by a disbelieving Saw.

K-2SO

Designed to serve as a security droid for the Empire, K-2SO was reprogrammed by Cassian and now works for the rebels. He is loyal, but not happy about it.

SAW GERRERA

A veteran of the Clone Wars, Saw was a friend of Jyn Erso's family. He taught Jyn to be a warrior as he waged war on the Empire using extreme terror tactics.

Tarkin was top dog on the Death Star in Episode IV, so...

WHO IS DIRECTOR ORSON KRENNIC?

He's a new bad guy with a cool cape. But where does Director Krennic fit in to the story of the Rogue One rebels?

WHO RUNS THE DEATH STAR IN *ROGUE ONE*?

When the movie begins, the Death Star falls under Krennic's jurisdiction as Director of the Empire's Advanced Weapons Research Division. But as soon as the battle station proves its effectiveness, it ceases to be just a research project and becomes the most valuable piece of real estate in the galaxy. So it's no surprise that Grand Moff Tarkin, one of the most powerful governors in the Empire, chooses that moment to pull rank and claim command of the Death Star for himself. Krennic cries foul, but that doesn't get you very far in an evil Empire.

WHAT'S KRENNIC'S LINK TO THE ERSO FAMILY?

Krennic knew Galen Erso in his youth and later tricked the scientist into helping design the Death Star. When Galen found out he was building a weapon, he fled into hiding with his wife, Lyra, and their daughter, Jyn. Krennic vowed that he would track Galen down and put him back to work.

ORSON KRENNIC

WHY DOES HE GO TO SEE DARTH VADER?

It's not a social call. The Sith Lord orders Krennic to come and explain why word of the Death Star is getting out around the galaxy (clue: people will talk if you blow up a city.) Instead of fearing an audience with Vader, ambitious Krennic sees it as a chance to curry favor with the Emperor. When he asks the Dark Lord to put in a good word for him, Vader makes him literally choke on his request.

Even Sith Lords have a sense of humor! When Darth Vader takes Krennic's breath away, he warns him not to choke on his aspirations.

WHAT'S HE DOING AT THE BASE ON SCARIF?

With Vader's Force choke still fresh in his mind (and throat), Krennic is eager to ensure the Death Star project hasn't been compromised further. He goes to the security complex where the Death Star plans are held, to personally ensure their safety, and to check whether Galen Erso left clues that revealed the project's existence. Unfortunately for him, his eternal rival Grand Moff Tarkin is not far behind, and has plans of his own for dealing with the problem…

Krennic and Jyn Erso go way back, to when she was a small girl and her father worked on Krennic's "Project Celestial Power."

WHY DOES HE WEAR THAT COOL CAPE?

Unlike most of the high-ranking officers in the Empire, Krennic isn't a posh guy from a privileged background. He probably feels like the cape gives him a touch of class. And given that Darth Vader wears one all the time, no one's really going to argue with that, are they?

In the dog-eat-dog Empire, Krennic should have known better than to invite Grand Moff Tarkin to see the Death Star in action.

BATTLE OF SCARIF
MADE SIMPLE

The battle that began the Galactic Civil War and marked the beginning of the Rebel Alliance's ultimate victory over the Empire. Without Scarif, the Empire might have stood forever.

REBELS

NEBULON-B ESCORT FRIGATES

PROFUNDITY

HAMMERHEAD CORVETTES

GHOST

X-WINGS

Y-WINGS

U-WINGS

WHO'S FIGHTING WHO?
A rebel strike team infiltrates the Imperial base on Scarif while the rebel fleet takes on Imperial ships in space above the planet.

CR90 CORVETTES

SHIELD ZONE

SCARIF

STAR DESTROYERS

TIE FIGHTERS

SHIELD GATE

EMPIRE

WHY ARE THEY FIGHTING?

The strike team on Scarif intend to steal the plans to the Death Star so it can be destroyed by the Rebel Alliance. The rebel fleet above must open or destroy the shield gate protecting Scarif so that the plans can be transmitted from the surface.

WHO WINS?

The rebels lose everyone on the Rogue One strike team when the Death Star vaporizes the Citadel base. However, getting the plans is a huge victory for the Rebel Alliance.

KEY MOMENT

HEAD-TO-HEAD—Rebel leader Admiral Raddus orders a Hammerhead corvette to ram a disabled Star Destroyer into another, causing them to crash into the shield gate, destroying it.

BATTLE IN A NUTSHELL

The rebels succeed in stealing the plans for the Death Star, giving them hope in their quest to defeat the Empire. However, it is also the beginning of the Galactic Civil War—with much suffering and loss to come.

EPISODE VIII:
THE LAST JEDI

*"I only know one truth.
It's time for the
Jedi to end."*

LUKE SKYWALKER

It's time for the next chapter in the saga, so…

WHAT DO I NEED TO KNOW?

Starkiller Base has been destroyed! The war against the First Order is over, right? Nope. The bad guys have come looking for revenge, and with the New Republic gone, things have just taken a turn for the worse. Only Rey, hopefully with some cool new Jedi powers, stands a chance of stopping them.

WHERE IS REY?

Rey has traveled to the mysterious planet of Ahch-To, where Luke Skywalker has been living in exile. She hopes that she can convince him to join the Resistance, and help her understand and harness the strange powers that she feels growing within her. Faced with this legendary hero, Rey might find that Luke challenges her expectations...

WHAT NOW FOR THE RESISTANCE?

The Resistance won the battle, but not the war, and now the First Order knows where they are hiding. Evacuation will likely be the order of the day, and the Resistance will have to find a new home to set up for the coming struggle. They will look to General Organa for guidance.

WILL LUKE ACTUALLY SAY ANYTHING IN THIS ONE?

Yes! Although years of living alone on a cold, wet, and rocky island may mean he has to brush up on his social skills, and his hermit lifestyle could make Rey's task slightly awkward. Luke's reaction to Rey's growing Force powers will obviously play a crucial role in the story.

Leia knows that the Resistance's only hope is to hold out long enough for rescue.

WHAT HAS HAPPENED TO FINN?

Finn had a nasty encounter with a lightsaber during his duel with Kylo Ren. Luckily, it seems Kylo didn't hit anything vital, and with the help of a suit full of healing bacta, Finn should be up and about in no time. He's going to wonder what has happened to Rey in his absence.

WHO IS ROSE?

Rose serves as a technician in the Resistance. She is tough, smart, and loyal, but she has a tragic past that she prefers to keep hidden. Thrown together by a twist of fate, Rose and Finn will be spending a lot of time in each other's company.

LUKE'S ISLAND HIGHLIGHTS

Caretakers
Strange and enigmatic creatures, the Caretakers look after the crumbling ruins that dot the island.

Porgs
Small, bird-like porgs are the island's most adorable inhabitants. Cute? Definitely. Tasty? Maybe…

Huts
What Luke's stone-built home lacks in comfort, it makes up for in privacy.

Sea Views
Although Rey won't have time to stop and admire them, Ahch-To's vistas are undeniably grand.

Well that's got me excited! So...

WHAT SHOULD I LOOK OUT FOR?

The Force Awakens *was a wild ride. New heroes?* **Check**. *New villains?* **Obviously**. *A story of hope in the darkest of times?* **Always**. *A cute little droid that rolls along like a ball?* **You betcha**. *With that in mind, what could possibly make* The Last Jedi *as awesome? Well...*

BIG EXPLOSIONS

The Resistance fleet doesn't have the firepower of the First Order, but these bombers help to even the odds. They are full of proton bombs, which rain down in a lovely curtain of destruction. Anyone on the receiving end is going to have a really, *really* bad day.

WEALTHY ALIENS

Canto Bight is one of the wealthiest, glitziest places in the galaxy—think Monte Carlo, but in *Star Wars*. Politicians, business magnates, career criminals, arms dealers, and other assorted characters come here to show off their riches and bet in the casinos.

SPACE HORSES

Graceful and majestic creatures, fathiers are prized across the galaxy for their ability to run *extremely* fast. The Canto Bight casinos exploit them for competitive (and highly popular) races.

GORILLA WALKERS

Say hello to the AT-M6. Short for "All Terrain Megacaliber 6," this beast is the biggest walker in the First Order arsenal. As well as the huge cannon on its back, its armored knuckles pack a massive punch.

SCARY BODYGUARDS

Supreme Leader Snoke's personal guards, the Praetorians' red armor harks back to Emperor Palpatine's Royal Guard. Highly trained and carrying unique weapons, these guys are not to be trifled with.

WELL THAT'S JUST CRAIT!

Site of an abandoned rebel base, Crait is a geologically unique world. A thin layer of salt covers the dark red minerals beneath. When the salt layer is broken, the pristine surface is stained the color of blood... All very dramatic.

ANOTHER NEW TIE FIGHTER...

Kylo Ren's customized TIE fighter, the TIE Silencer combines the agility of a starfighter with the hitting power of a bomber. When matched with Kylo's Force abilities, this is one ship you don't want to see heading in your direction.

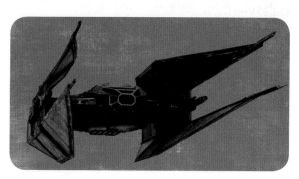

"Light.
Darkness.
A Balance."

REY

GLOSSARY

AT-AT
An All Terrain Armored Transport (AT-AT) is a four-legged combat walker used by the Galactic Empire.

Clone trooper
A soldier created to serve in the Republic's army. All clone troopers are genetically identical.

The Clone Wars
A troubled time in galactic history when the Republic and the Separatists were at war.

Confederacy of Independent Systems
An alliance of star systems and trade bodies who wish to break away from the control of the Galactic Senate. Also known as the Separatist Alliance or Separatists.

Death Star
A mobile, sphere-shaped battle station the size of a small moon, built by the Empire.

Droid
A robot built to carry out a variety of duties.

Episode
Any movie that centers on the story of the Skywalker family.

The First Order
A powerful army, formed after the downfall of the Galactic Empire.

The Force
A mysterious energy that flows through the galaxy and all living things. It has a light side and a dark side.

Galactic Empire
A group of worlds ruled by the unelected Emperor Palpatine.

Galactic Republic
A group of worlds governed by an elected senate.

Galactic Senate
Elected representatives of all of the Republic's planets, who come together to pass laws.

Hyperdrive
A device that allows starships to travel at the speed of light.

Hyperspace
A parallel region of space through which starships pass when traveling faster than light.

Jedi Council
A group that looks after the running of the entire Jedi Order.

Jedi Knight
A member of the Jedi Order who has studied as a Padawan and has passed the Jedi trials.

Jedi Master
A rank for a Jedi Knight who has performed an exceptional deed or who serves on the Jedi Council.

Knights of Ren
A group of warriors loyal to Supreme Leader Snoke.

Kyber crystal
Force-attuned crystals that focus energy. Used to power lightsabers and both Death Stars.

Lightsaber
A sword-like weapon with a plasma blade used by the Jedi and Sith.

Lightspeed
The speed at which starships can travel through space.

Millennium Falcon
A highly modified light freighter starship piloted by Han Solo and, later, Rey.

New Republic
The new alliance formed from the Rebel Alliance after the collapse of the Galactic Empire.

Padawan
A youngling who is chosen to serve an apprenticeship with a Jedi Knight or Master.

Podracing
An extreme sport on Tatooine where competitors ride in chariots pulled by oversized engines.

Rebel Alliance
A group that opposes the rule of the Empire.

The Resistance
A group of rebels whose aim is to defeat the First Order.

Sith
An order of Force-sensitive beings who use the dark side of the Force for evil.

Starkiller Base
A mobile, weaponized planet used as the First Order's headquarters.

Stormtrooper
A soldier of the Galactic Empire and First Order.

Tauntaun
An animal native to the ice planet Hoth, used as a mount by the Rebel Alliance.

TIE fighter
An Imperial fighter spacecraft powered by twin ion engines.

Trade Federation
An influential association of business and trade bodies within the Republic.

Wampa
A fierce, yeti-like creature found on the planet Hoth.

X-wing
A starfighter that resembles an "X," used by the Rebel Alliance, New Republic, and Resistance.

Youngling
A Force-sensitive child in the first stages of Jedi training.

"May the Force be with you" is only the beginning...

STAR WARS QUOTES EVERYONE SHOULD KNOW

A catchy line can make its way through space in parsecs. These quotes have all entered our cultural consciousness, but remember where you heard them first. In a galaxy far, far, away...

"Laugh it up, fuzzball."
HAN SOLO, EPISODE V

"I'm one with the Force, the Force is with me."
CHIRRUT ÎMWE, ROGUE ONE

"So this is how liberty dies... with thunderous applause."
SENATOR PADMÉ, EPISODE III

"It's against my programming to impersonate a deity."
C-3PO, EPISODE VI

"Aren't you a little short for a stormtrooper?"
PRINCESS LEIA, EPISODE IV

"Do. Or do not. There is no try."
YODA, EPISODE V

"Fear leads to anger. Anger leads to hate. Hate leads to suffering."
YODA, EPISODE I

"Chewie, we're home."
HAN SOLO, EPISODE VII

"He's more machine now than man. Twisted and evil."
OBI-WAN KENOBI, EPISODE VI

"I love you."

LEIA TO HAN, EPISODE V

"I know."

HAN TO LEIA, EPISODE V

"That's not how the Force works!"

HAN SOLO, EPISODE VII

"That lightsaber... it belongs to me!"

KYLO REN, EPISODE VII

"And you, young Skywalker, we shall watch your career with great interest."

SENATOR PALPATINE, EPISODE I

"Impressive. Most impressive."

DARTH VADER, EPISODE V

"You will never find a more wretched hive of scum and villainy."

OBI-WAN KENOBI, EPISODE IV

SAY WHAT? "I have a bad feeling about this," or a version of it, is spoken in every Star Wars *movie.*

"Henceforth, you shall be known as Darth...Vader!"

EMPEROR PALPATINE, EPISODE III

"You rebel scum!"

IMPERIAL OFFICER, LIEUTENANT RENZ, EPISODE VI

"Let the Wookiee win."

C-3PO, EPISODE IV

"These aren't the droids you're looking for."

OBI-WAN KENOBI, EPISODE IV

"So who talks first? You talk first? I talk first?"

POE DAMERON, EPISODE VII

"Size matters not."

YODA, EPISODE V

PRONUNCIATION GUIDE

Ahsoka Tano
ah-SOE-kah TAA-noe

Alderaan
ALL-der-rahn

Anakin Skywalker
AN-na-kin SKY-walk-er

Asajj Ventress
ah-SAAZJ VENN-tress

Astromech
ASS-trow-meck

AT-AT
AY-tee-AY-tee

Baze Malbus
bayz MAL-bus

Beru Lars
beh-ROO larz

Boba Fett
BOW-bah fet

Bodhi Rook
BOW-dee rook

C-3PO
see-THREE-pee-oh

Cassian Andor
CASS-ee-an AN-dor

Chewbacca
choo-BAC-ah

Chirrut Îmwe
CHEER-utt IMM-way

Cliegg Lars
kleeg larz

Coruscant
coh-ROO-sont

Count Dooku
count DOO-koo

Dagobah
DAGG-oe-baa

Darth Maul
darth mawl

Darth Sidious
darth SID-ee-us

Darth Vader
darth VAY-der

D'Qar
duh-KAR

Endor
EN-door

Ewok
EE-wok

Ezra Bridger
EZZ-ruh BRIH-jer

Galen Erso
GAY-lun ERR-so

Garazeb Orrelios (Zeb)
GAIR-uh-ZEBB or-RELL-ee-ose (zebb)

General Grievous
gen-er-al GREE-vuss

Geonosis
gee-oe-NOE-sis

Greedo
GREE-doh

Hera Syndulla
HAIR-uh sinn-DUE-luh

Jabba the Hutt
JA-ber the hut

Jakku
jah-KOO

Jango Fett
JAN-go fet

Jar Jar Binks
jar jar BINKS

Jawa
JAH-wah

Jedha
JED-uh

Jedi
JEH-die

Jyn Erso
gin ERR-so

Kamino
kuh-MEE-no

Kanan Jarrus
KAY-nenn JAIR-uss

Kashyyyk
kaa-SHEEK

Lando Calrissian
LAN-doh cal-RISS-ee-un

Leia Organa
LAY-ah or-GAH-nah

Mace Windu
mase WIN-doo

Mon Calamari
monn caa-laa-MAR-ee

Mustafar
MOOSE-tah-far

Naboo
nah-BOO

Neimoidian
nay-MOI-dee-ann

Nute Gunray
noot GUNN-ray

Obi-Wan Kenobi
OH-bee-waan
ken-OH-bee

Padawan
PAH-duh-waan

Padmé Amidala
PAD-may a-mee-DA-ler

Palpatine
PAL-puh-teen

Poe Dameron
poe DAM-err-on

Qui-Gon Jinn
KWY-gonn jin

Sabine Wren
suh-BEEN renn

Sarlacc
SAR-lak

Sebulba
se-BULL-bah

Scarif
SKAR-iff

Shmi Skywalker
shmee SKY-walk-er

Takodana
tack-oh-DAAN-uh

Tatooine
ta-too-EEN

Watto
WAT-toe

Yavin 4
YAH-vin four

Yoda
YOH-da

Zam Wesell
zamm WESS-ull

INDEX

Main entries are in **bold**

A

AATs (Armoured Assault Tanks) 105, 119
Abrams, J.J. 11, 166
Ackbar, Admiral 83, 85
action figures 12, 13
Alderaan 48, 49, 50, 55, 56, 57, 99
aliens 18–19
Amidala, Padmé 20, 22, **114–15**, 117
    Episode I 17, 104–7, 111–12, 118–19
    Episode II 121–5, 127–9, 131
    Episode III 75, 134–7, 142–3
Andor, Cassian 172, 173, 174, 175, 178, 179
animals 19
Antilles, Wedge 68, 79
asteroid field 68, 70, 72
astromech droids 24
AT-AT walkers 26, 68, 70, 72, 73, 79, 164
Aurebesh 19

B

bacta tanks 73
Bane, Cad 151
banthas 19
Basic 19
Bast 61
battle droids 53, 123
BB-8 20, 156, 158, 159, 166–7
Beed 112
Bespin 15, 76
Binks, Jar Jar 104, 105, 106, 107, **108–9**
books 9, 12, 17, 153
box office chart 13
Bridger, Ezra 152, 153

C

C-3PO 19, 20, 89
    Episode IV 48, 50, 51, 55
    Episode V 69, 71
    Episode VI 84, 86, 88, 89
    Rogue One 177
Calrissian, Lando 20, 69, 71, **76–7**, 81, 87, 153, 177
Cass 61
Cave of Evil 74
Chewbacca 18, 20
    Episode IV 48, 51
    Episode V 68–71
    Episode VI 84–5, 93
    Episode VII 156–9
    Rogue One 177
Chopper 152, 153
chronology 44–5, 176
clone army 122, 123, 129
clone troopers 42, 53, 130, 137, 144

Clone Wars 35, 42, 52, 126, 131, 150–1
clones 144–5, 150
Cloud City 69, 71, 75, 76, 77, 80, 99
Cody 150
combat droids 127
comics 9, 17
computer-generated characters 109
Confederacy of Independent Systems 126, 129
Coruscant 15, 35, 56, 105, 106
Coruscant, Battle of 134, **146–7**
Crumb, Salacious B. 93
cyborgs 135, 137, 138, 139

D

Dagobah 68, 70, 74, 84, 86
Dameron, Poe 20, 156, 157, 158, 159, 167, 168, 169
the dark side 30, **33**, 40, 63, 74, 90
    Anakin and 61, 100, 108, 135, **142–3**, 151
    Luke and 74, 75, 85, **90–1**
"Darth" 41, 116
Darth Vader (Marvel Comics) 17
Dathomir 117
Death Star 25, 48, **56–7**, 60, 65, 180–1
    destruction of 49, 51, 65, 78, 96
    fatal flaw 51, 64, 96, 172, 174
    plans 50, 51, 53, 54, **55**, 123, 173, 175, 177, 181, 183
Death Star II 84, 85, 86, 87, 94, 95, 96–7, 160
death troopers 43
Dooku, Count 123–7, 131, 134, 136–7, 139, 140, 146–7
D'Qar 157, 168
droid army 130–1, 144
droid control ship 105, 118, 119
droid tri-fighters 134
droids 19

E

Eadu 172, 175
Empire see Galactic Empire
The Empire Strikes Back see Episode V
Endor 15, 85, 86, 87, 97, 99
Endor, Battle of 85, **94–5**
Episode I: *The Phantom Menace* 11, 13, 16, 28, 44, 102–19
Episode II: *Attack of the Clones* 11, 13, 17, 28, 44, 45, 120–31
Episode III: *Revenge of the Sith* 11, 13, 17, 28, 44, 45, 132–47
Episode IV: *A New Hope* 9, 11, 12, 13, 16, 29, 44, 46–65, 70, 176, 177
Episode V: *The Empire Strikes Back* 11, 13, 16, 29, 44, 45, 52, 66–81
Episode VI: *Return of the Jedi* 11, 13, 16, 29, 44, 45, 63, 82–101
Episode VII: *The Force Awakens* 11, 13, 17, 29, 44, 45, 53, 109, 154–69
Episode VIII: *The Last Jedi* 9, 11, 13, 16, 17, 29, 44, 45, 53, 177, 184–91
Episode IX 11, 177

Erso, Galen 172, 173, 174, 175, 180, 181
Erso, Jyn 20, 171, 172–5, 178, 179, 180, 181
Erso, Lyra 172, 174, 180
Ewoks 19, 85, 86, 87, **88–9**, 94, 95, 101, 160
Executor 97

F

fambaas 105
fan base 9, 12
Fett, Boba 21, 68, 69, 71, 84, 86, 87
Fett, Jango 122, 123, 124, 125
Finn 20, 38, 155, 156, 157, 158, 159, 166, 167
First Order 29, 43, 158, 159, **160–1**, 162, 163, 167, 168–9
FN-2187 see Finn
the Force 22, **30–1**, 34, 35, 98–9, 165
    ghosts 62, 63, 87
    light and dark side **32–3**, 40, 63
The Force Awakens see Episode VII
Ford, Harrison 58
Forest Moon of Endor 85, 97
Fortuna, Bib 93

G

Galactic Civil War 79, 94–5, 182–3
Galactic Empire 28–9, 43, 49, 53, 58, 64–5, 78–9, 94–5, 160, 182–3
Galactic Republic 14, 28–9, 42, 123–31, 134, 136, 137, 145, 146–7
Galactic Senate 28, 105–7, **110–11**, 114, 118, 123, 124, 126, 128–9, 140, 145, 161
galaxy, *Star Wars* 14–15
    inhabitants 18–19
Gasgano 113
Geonosis 15, 25, 122, 123, 124, 125, 127
Geonosis, Battle of 123, **130–1**
Gerrera, Saw 17, 153, 172, 174, 179
The *Ghost* 152
Grand Army of the Republic 129
Grand Inquisitor 153
Grand Masters, Jedi 34, 36
Graveyard of Giants 164
Greedo 58–9
Grievous, General 134, 136, 137, **138–9**, 146–7, 150
Guardians of the Whills 178
Gungans 19, 105, 106, 107, 108, 109, 115, 118–19
Gunray, Nute 110, 111, 118, 119, 127
Guo, Mars 113

H

Hosnian Prime 161, 168
Hoth 15, 68, 70, 72–3
Hoth, Battle of 70, **78–9**
humans 18–19
Hutt Clan 93
Hux 169
hyperdrive 24
hyperspace 24–5, 56

I, J, K

Imperial Archive Facility 57
Imperial era 28–9
Imperial Senate 53
Îmwe, Chirrut 173, 174, 175, 178
Indiana Jones 11
Industrial Light & Magic (ILM) 53
Invisible Hand 134, 146
ion cannons 73
Jabba the Hutt 21, 48, 58–9, 69, 71, 84, 86–7, 91, 92–3, 113
Jabba's Palace 84
Jakku 15, 156, 158, 164, 165, 167
Jarrus, Kanan 152, 153
Jawa 19, 55
Jawaese 19
Jedha 57, 172, 174
Jedha City 57, 172, 174
Jedi 8, 28, 29, 32, **34–7**, 38, 62, 63, 104–5, 116–17, 125, 128, 130–1, 135, 137, 141, 144–5, 147, 151, 160
Jedi Council 34, 105, 107, 123, 134
Jedi starfighters 134
Jedi Temple 35, 135, 137
Jerjerrod, Moff 96
Jinn, Qui-Gon 63, 104, 105, 106, 107, 109, 112, 117
Johnson, Rian 11
Jones, James Earl 81
K-2SO 173, 174, 175, 179
Kaleesh 138, 139
Kamino 122
Kanata, Maz 109, 156, 159, 165
Kasdan, Lawrence 11
Kashyyyk 134
Kennedy, Kathleen 11
Kenobi, Obi-Wan 21, 31, 34, 38, 42, **54–5**, **62–3**
    Episode I 104–7, 117
    Episode II 122–5, 131
    Episode III 133–7, 139, 146
    Episode IV 48–51, 54–6, 61–3
    Episode V 70–1
    Episode VI 99–101
    Star Wars: The Clone Wars 150–1
Kershner, Irving 11
Kessel Run 25
Knights, Jedi 34, 35, 37, 128
Knights of Ren 163
Kowakian monkey-lizards 93
Krennic, Orson 172, 174, 175, **180–1**
kyber crystals 38, 39, 56, 57

L

LAAT/i landers 123
languages 19
Lars, Beru 22
Lars, Cliegg 22
Lars, Owen 22, 55
The Last Jedi see Episode VIII
Legends 17
Leia Organa, Princess 21, 22, **54–5**, **98–9**
    Episode III 135, 137
    Episode IV 46, 48–51, 53–5
    Episode V 68–9, 70–1, 79, 80
    Episode VI 84–7, 93, 98–9
    Episode VII 157–9, 161–3, 167
    Rogue One 173
    Star Wars Rebels 153

Editors Ruth Amos, Natalie Edwards,
Ben Ffrancon Davies, David Fentiman,
Katy Lennon, Eleanor Rose
Designers Owen Bennett, Rosamund Bird,
Stefan Georgiou, Ian Midson, Mark Penfound,
Jade Wheaton, Abi Wright
Senior Pre-Production Producer Jennifer Murray
Senior Producer Mary Slater
Managing Editor Sarah Harland
Managing Art Editor Guy Harvey
Publisher Julie Ferris
Art Director Lisa Lanzarini
Publishing Director Simon Beecroft

Edited for DK by Simon Hugo

With thanks to Sadie Smith and Lisa Stock for additional editorial
assistance, and David McDonald for design assistance.

For Lucasfilm
Senior Editor Brett Rector
Image Unit Shahana Alam, Nicole LaCoursiere, Gabrielle
Levenson, Tim Mapp, Bryce Pinkos, Erik Sanchez, and Newell Todd
Story Group Leland Chee, Pablo Hidalgo, and Matt Martin
Creative Director of Publishing Michael Siglain

First American Edition, 2017
Published in the United States by DK Publishing
345 Hudson Street, New York, NY 10014

Page design copyright © 2017 Dorling Kindersley Limited
DK, a division of Penguin Random House LLC
17 18 19 20 21 10 9 8 7 6 5 4 3 2
002–306465–September/2017

Published in Great Britain by
Dorling Kindersley Limited.

A catalog record for this book is available
from the Library of Congress.

ISBN: 978-1-4654-6521-4

DK books are available at special discounts when
purchased in bulk for sales promotions, premiums,
fund-raising, or educational use. For details, contact:
DK Publishing Special Markets,
345 Hudson Street, New York, New York 10014
SpecialSales@dk.com

Printed and bound in the USA

A WORLD OF IDEAS:
SEE ALL THERE IS TO KNOW

www.dk.com
www.starwars.com